Get **more** out of libraries

Please return or renew this item by the last date shown.

You can renew online at www.hants.gov.uk/library

Or by phoning   0300 555 1387

 Hampshire
County Council

First published in Great Britain in 2016 by Wayland
Text © Rosalind Jana, 2016

ISBN: 978 0 7502 8732 6
10 9 8 7 6 5 4 3

Printed in England

Wayland
An imprint of Hachette Children's Group
Part of Hodder & Stoughton
Carmelite House
50 Victoria Embankment
London EC4Y 0DZ

An Hachette UK Company
www.hachette.co.uk
www.hachettechildrens.co.uk

Editorial Director: Debbie Foy
Senior Commissioning Editor: Joyce Bentley
Copy Editor: Sorrel Wood
Editor: Elizabeth Brent
Designer: Claire Yeo
Consultants: Luke Jefferies and Justin Hancock

CONTENTS

ACKNOWLEDGEMENTS

Huge thanks to the Wayland team – especially to Joyce Bentley for first believing in the idea. Also to Debbie Foy, Sorrel Wood and Elizabeth Brent for everything they did to help tailor that idea into a fully-fledged book.

Big appreciation for my agent Diana Beaumont. She is fierce and fabulous and I feel lucky to know her. Also for my parents - thanks for putting up with my endless phone calls.

Also to Susie Wynne Wilson, Justin Hancock, and Luke Jefferies for offering their expert opinions.

Thanks also to the excellent handful of friends who joined me for coffee-fuelled chats about mental health, sense of self, teenage experiences and plenty else.

Finally a massive THANK YOU to all the brilliant people who talked with me whilst I was writing this. To the older women who shared their wisdom, and the 50+ teens and twenty-somethings who opened up about their lives and thoughts: you're all wonderful. They didn't all end up in the book, but every single one of those conversations influenced what I ended up putting down on these pages. It was both a pleasure and privilege to chat with all of you.

START HERE

Hey. I'm Rosalind.

Chances are, we've never met. If we *were* chatting face to face though, we'd probably be sitting in a café. I love nothing better than bouncing ideas around with someone else, setting the world to rights over a cup of coffee. Let's assume this chat had been organised so we could talk about 'being teenage' ... whatever that means. I'm only just out of my teens – I recently walked through the next door into my 20s. This book began as a seed of an idea when I was 17.

Where would our conversation go? Maybe we'd end up talking about the stress of exams, or the delights of dressing just for you, or unravel the ins and outs of a family argument. No doubt we'd jump around from one topic to another: you or your friend's trouble with anxiety one minute, to disappointing first kisses the next. Who knows? Hopefully I'd be able to shed some light, or even offer a sprinkle of advice.

Sadly, not every conversation can take place in person. But that's where this book comes in. When I began work on it, I thought a lot about what shaped me as a teenager. Such a mix of both unusual and normal stuff. I was scouted as a model age 13; began my blog, and discovered the wonder of charity shops the year after. At 15, my spine stopped growing upward and began curving to the side which took me out of school for an operation and months of physio. I started seriously thinking about writing, and my first article in *Vogue* was published when I was 16. When I was 17 my dad, the one I knew and loved, disappeared for six months – his depression stole him away.

Those are the big moments, some wonderful, some awful. In between all of that there were bitchy friends, terrible times when I thought I'd be single forever, and one rather unfortunate drunken evening where I threw up on everything, including my parents ... I also spent a fair amount of time trying to work out what being a teen really is, and what it does to us all. Everyone is different, but there is a lot we may end up sharing: the way you see your body, or the agony of fancying someone who doesn't feel the same way.

I also know how complicated 'it', this thing of being a teen, can be. In some senses, I had a fantastic time as a teenager. My ever-so-brilliant family always gave me love, support and confidence in my own abilities, I began a successful blog that I still adore working on, became a model, won the *Vogue* Talent Writing competition, and ended up at a university I love.

However, at times I was also trying very hard not to burst into tears – especially at school. I was unsure of myself in all sorts of ways. Now I know I wasn't alone in that. When I began talking to other teens and women I admired, nearly all of them admitted to having struggled, alongside the brilliant stuff. My thoughts, and theirs, are collected here. I hope you enjoy the results!

With love,

Rosalind

I ~~LOVE~~ ~~HATE~~ LOVE THE WAY I LOOK

1

AND SO IT BEGAN ... WITH BOOBS

Once, standing in the lunch queue at secondary school, my friends turned to discussing which parts of their body they'd change if they could. I was asked, and before I could reply, one of my so-called friends butted in: 'You'd want bigger boobs, yeah?' I mumbled a 'maybe' and left it there. Since the age of seven or eight I'd thought an hourglass figure was the height (or maybe width) of beauty, but standing in that lunch queue at the age of 14, my body was still much more of a line than a curve.

In spite of my own misgivings about my body shape, I'd been signed to a top model agency a few months previously. Barely into puberty, I was scouted at a shopping event and invited to London. I felt like Alice, arriving at the offices, walking down the mirrored corridor to enter what I thought was Wonderland. Polaroids were taken, my measurements noted. As a young teenager, all bony knees and sharp elbows, my body fitted sample size clothes perfectly.

I thought I was being handed the key to a new future. This agency worked with the brands I saw in *Vogue*: Chanel, Burberry, Prada. One day, I was told, *they* might notice me. As a newly signed model, it was this potential that thrilled me the most – the opportunity of sudden transformation if I caught the eye of a leading magazine or designer.

Now I wonder if, particularly for teens, modelling seems exciting because it's one of the few ways young women can seemingly be transported into another life. What other industry finds a leggy 14 year old, tells her they love her look and asks if she fancies being dressed up in designer clothes?

The reality for me was that education (thankfully) came first. I had to wait until I turned 16 to do catwalk and the serious editorial stuff. For most people it's an exciting birthday – the first proper whiff of independence, the sense that you're on the way to growing up and, eventually, leaving home. For me, it had the extra attraction of being a possible entry-point into proper work.

Until that day I had to be happy with the occasional job during holidays or on weekends. I was always accompanied by my mum, who tirelessly organised train tickets and tube routes. She was brilliant, considering her role usually meant sitting at the back of the studio with a book.

These early shoots were a mix of Japanese fashion mags, the occasional lookbook for a designer (the images used to showcase their latest collection to buyers), and even a trip to Paris, the Eiffel Tower visible from the balcony of the shoot location. The thrill of being surrounded by a big team was heightened by a clothes rail full of Chanel, Hermès, Céline and Stella McCartney, at a point where I cared deeply about those labels. The Paris shoot came closest to what I'd previously imagined modelling might entail, providing an experience I couldn't imagine getting in any other way. Here I was, being taken seriously, by grown-ups. *In Paris.*

Yet in between the odd bit of excitement, there were months of coming back from school asking, 'Any emails? Any news?' Mum's answer was nearly always no. Perhaps I was naïve in my enthusiasm. Naïve, but human. We all tend to imagine our futures as successful. Every new model wants to be the next Kate Moss or Naomi Campbell. I certainly did.

That innocence was inevitable. At 13, there was no way I could enter the industry fully aware of what it was like. But now that I'm a bit older, and have had a chance to learn more, there are elements of the fashion industry that horrify me. Using young teens to sell clothes to adult women, for example, or telling those teens once they reach 16 that the slightest increase in hip or waist measurements is unacceptable and may lose them work.

At that point though, I still defined myself by the reactions of those around me, meaning that the agency's interest was a welcome contrast to school, where my skinniness was seen as unattractive. Being signed to that top agency gave me short-lived status among (and a scattering of nasty comments from) my peers at an age when I craved acceptance. What's more, I thought it might open doors in the future.

In reality it was also tough. I didn't really get anywhere: never booked a high-profile campaign, spent a lot of time frustrated at my seeming lack of work. I'm not ungrateful, but think it's important to note that modelling only provides a glamorous lifestyle for a select few. Most models aren't showered with free clothes and holidays. I walked away from my first agency with the grand total of £27. Reality rarely matches the glitz.

But the media continues to present modelling in one of two ways. The first is: Look how wonderful and brilliant this all is! The opportunities! The travel! Here are some smiley young girls with perfect teeth and good hair with gushy quotes about their job! The second is: This is evil and disgusting. Models are *all* anorexic. I hate fashion, and you should too. If you don't? How superficial *are* you?

There's no middle ground, nowhere to say, hey, modelling can be great – but it's not the be-all and end-all.

In recent years modelling's been a more rewarding occasional career for me, and I've met amazing people through it: photographers, stylists, designers and make-up artists. Without the modelling, I wouldn't have got to where I am now. However, I'm fully aware of the flaws of the industry and I hope to carry on shouting about all of that unfairness for a long time to come.

A TWIST IN THE TALE

Unfortunately, before reaching that magic number 16, my sprouting career got cut off. Shortly before I turned 15, I was diagnosed with severe scoliosis, a condition that causes twisting of the spine. It was idiopathic, meaning cause unknown. As a teen girl, I was among those most likely to be affected. X-rays revealed a spine that looked like a wobbly question mark. As it curved further, my torso did too. My right shoulder blade stuck out like a triangle, my ribcage shifting until a lump was visible under my skin. As my back twisted, the pain increased until it was almost unbearable.

Clad in sample size clothing, my body had been celebrated: now it felt out of place. I became self-conscious, hyper-aware of how others might be viewing me. At school I hated the bulge of my shoulder blade, the hump of my ribs under my sweatshirt. At home I wore big shirts, trying to hide any sign of my spine. But my attempts to pretend it didn't exist weren't always successful.

Once I went shopping for a new bra. There were mirrors on three sides of the changing room cubicle and my back was on show from every angle. I saw it more clearly than in months. Reflections bounced. I sobbed in the car on the way home. What I'd seen was something that, to me, seemed so far beyond what 'normal' was meant to look like – what *I* was meant to look like.

In the space of six months my spine went from having a 56-degree curve (imagine zero degrees being a straight line) to curving by 80 degrees. The first consultant – a bearded, red-faced man who'd sternly told me that, having started my periods, I wouldn't grow any more, thus it wouldn't get worse and so I could go away and live my life – was wrong. I grew (of course I grew, I was 14!). It got worse. Much worse. A summer growth spurt fed into the curve to the point that, rather than getting taller, I actually lost an inch in height.

The only answer was surgery – a six-hour operation during which the surgeon cut through to reveal my vertebrae, inserted two metal rods, one on either side, and attached them via screws and hooks into my spine. Artificial bone graft was packed into gaps cleared between my vertebrae, in order to slowly fuse the top half of my spine into a solid bone mass over the following six months. The rods were just there to scaffold it during the process. My curvature was reduced from 80 degrees to 22 degrees, a crescent moon being straightened out to a gentle curve, and I was Alice again – gaining several inches in a single day.

The agony of that first week in hospital is something I still struggle to recall. The night after the operation I was in Intensive Care, and I flew high on morphine. When it wore off in the morning, my back felt full of lead. It pulled me down, made me heavy. It hurt until I could think of nothing but how to get through each minute in turn. My hours were marked by breathing in and breathing out. Sleep was the golden space where pain could be escaped. For the first few days I repeatedly threw up, kept nothing down, not even water. I had to call someone to be moved onto my side or to return me to lying on my back.

I could hardly walk – something I would have to relearn – and relied on others to wash, feed and look after me. It was slow. My body wasn't quite mine any more. I owned the pain alone, but gave up other parts to doctors, nurses and parents. I took my pills and saw the IV do its work, let them take my blood each morning and trusted in their care. Life was suspended for a little while. Everything disappeared but the desire to get well.

It was worth it. I had two months off school, but I recovered, with a neck-to-waist scar to mark the experience. Short-term pain for a lifetime's gain. I love that scar now. It has faded to a faint pearly, puckered line, an incredible souvenir of that time.

Inevitably, this whole process altered my views on appearance. Going from having a 'model body' to a very twisted one, to something slightly wonky, was bewildering. I made the decision to leave my model agency shortly after. Several years on, my shape has changed again, although not due to my spine. This shape is healthy. It works. It's more curved in conventional ways, less bony – in proportion to my height. My back still aches, but it's functional. I can walk, swim, cycle and dance into the early hours.

Being no longer a sample size 6–8, I don't do mainstream modelling, but I do still model from time to time. I'm signed to another agency; who are awesome because they represent me as a person with achievements, rather than just as a face.

LOGIC HAS NOTHING TO DO WITH IT

If you ask me about how things have turned out, I'll say that I'm fine with this new body, that I'd rather eat well and exercise than count calories. That's true most of the time. But despite being grateful for a body that lets me go about my day, I still get hang-ups. My back remains a little lopsided, the right shoulder sticking out further than the left. Often I wish I had a smaller, less uneven ribcage. As much as I would hate to admit it, there's still the odd day when I feel immensely unconfident in my appearance.

For a while I'd constantly compare my current self with images taken several years previously, back when skinny jeans sagged over my hips. I'd hold myself up to my own prepubescent-looking body. Obviously doing so was, and is, ridiculous. But that's the problem with internal standards. They're *not* logical. For me, those years of being praised for my skinniness meant that, with a slightly larger dress size, my mind couldn't help sounding a note of dissatisfaction whenever I looked in the mirror. And the fact I knew this was stupid only made it worse.

This contradiction between understanding that self-worth shouldn't be based on physical looks, and the fact that it still is at times, isn't unique. Lots of people know that the fashion industry and the media present a completely warped image of 'normal' but would still quite like to change their own appearance in some way, regardless of how other people actually see them.

What I hope this demonstrates is that (a) If you wish your looks could be changed somehow, you're not alone, you're in the majority; and (b) Even if you hope you're beyond all that, you're not then doing something wrong if you sometimes feel a little twinge about your appearance.

I know I've been incredibly lucky in many ways, but sometimes I do still wish I was just a little thinner. Just a bit. Not much. And only if I could keep the boobs.

WHO ARE YOU COMPARING YOURSELF TO?

I can only talk about modelling from a position in front of the camera thanks to a strange combination of genetics and the views of our current society. Not so much right place, right time as right looks, right decade.

Standards of beauty are so much more diverse than the fashion world might have you think, yet all sorts of visuals from adverts to social media continue to tell us that certain types of looks are valued above others, and that the best qualities are youth, slenderness and, most ridiculously, white skin.

> You don't realise when you're a kid that it's actually very tiring seeing magazines, billboards and movies where everyone is white.
>
> Kandace, 19

For those who don't match up, it's suggested something must be wrong. Thighs should be slimmed, frizzy hair straightened and smoothed. No matter how much a person fits the ideal 'look', there is always something that can be improved on, according to the media and advertising. As a teenager, this can be particularly tough.

Awareness of appearance starts young. There must be a million studies on how many young people are worried about how they look, or have thought about dieting within the last year, but these surveys just throw out numbers. They don't help us understand the real, human problems at the heart of people's lives. Statistics just give a sketch of how many teens feel they should be prettier, cuter, hotter. Whatever word you most identify with, the feeling is one of falling short.

What are we falling short of? Usual suspects include celebrities, models, actors, singers, bloggers and vloggers. Basically anyone in the public eye held up as an ideal of what's beautiful. A lot of them have similar body shapes.

Yet these women are also slated if they don't consistently meet those expectations: an unhealthy dose of double standards. Many magazines publish massively conflicting messages: how we need to be happy in our bodies, but vilify a celebrity who's still showing her post-baby weight; natural is best, but an actress's sweat marks or cellulite deserve to be highlighted with a disapproving circle; we should dress for ourselves, but are encouraged to snigger over photos of so-called frock disasters.

The faces and figures of well-known women are seen as fair game. Men have similar pressures: teen boys are presented with a choice between rippling muscles or boy-band handsome. But to be female and famous tends to bring with it a higher level of focus on looks – whether it's celebration, or judgement – which often completely overshadows their work. (Never mind the Oscar, what are you wearing?)

It raises so many questions. Why not focus on women's achievements rather than how much weight they've lost or put on? Or admire all shapes rather than reinforce the line between skinny and curvy, like the only two options are Kate Moss or Kim Kardashian? When are we going to stop using the phrase 'real women'? All women are real, unless they're robots.

This endless emphasis on looks intensifies at school. We're encouraged to copy that kind of comparison and criticism among our friends and peers. It's a tiring – and useless – form of competition. Appearance becomes another way to mark out who's cool and who's not, just another thing to bitch about.

> In my school there's this serious pressure to be skinny and pretty and wear the right clothes. People get judged for anything and everything.
>
> Celia, 15

Anxiety about the way you look can have serious consequences. Although eating disorders are caused by myriad things more damaging than celebrity gossip, the pressure to look a certain way definitely doesn't help matters. Georgina, 18, who was hospitalised for her anorexia at 16, pointed out, 'The whole drive to be thin fuels eating disorders because people compliment you. You go, oh that's brilliant, I'll do it again – and again, and again, and again.'

Some people are lucky and seem to be completely unfazed by any of society's demands about beauty and appearance. A few people might even scoff at us when we admit we're influenced by imagery and media commentary. But knowing there is more to life than how you look is only part of the story or the solution for most people. There *is* more to life. There's so much more. That doesn't mean it's weak to admit to being affected by it all – most of us are.

LOOKING POSITIVE

Here's a handful of places that counteract gossip and snark and have something interesting to say about appearance:

StyleLikeU
Their What's Underneath video project investigates the relationship each of us has with the mirror.

All Walks Beyond the Catwalk
Aiming to make the fashion industry more diverse: they're subversive, stylish and mean business. Bias alert: I've written lots for their blog.

Centre for Appearance Research
Although it's an academic site, the stats, videos and surveys will definitely make you think about the way we see ourselves.

Thandie Kay
A space for celebrating beauty – especially when it comes to women of colour – with a fun mix of interviews, make-up tutorials and personal essays.

Shape Your Culture
Turn here if you want to take action: Want to make a zine? Start a campaign? Question the negative images of women (and men) we see every day?

Adios Barbie
A sharp-talking and honest website covering disability, activism, the media, size, race, LGBT issues and more.

Josy Spooner: The Model Agent

As part of the Special Bookings department at Models 1, Josy negotiates shoots for individuals who have another string to their bow – actors, singers, bloggers, or, in my case, writers.

How has the modelling industry changed in the last 10 years?

The digital age has completely changed the way people shop and consume, so models are being overwhelmingly used for e-commerce work. While there is much more demand for this type of work, it's much less glamorous. What was once a two-week trip to an exotic destination to shoot 10 outfits is now 50 different looks shot in a studio in the Midlands.

There's also a lot more focus on models as personalities, they are often chosen for their fame and social media following. Many brands choose to work with a celebrity for their PR appeal.

What's your response to the idea that models represent an unattainable ideal of beauty?

Advertisers are able to tap into our insecurities by providing unrealistic imagery, which encourages us to consume more and more in an attempt to look as good as the picture.

The rise of social media and of celebrity culture has also blurred the lines between what's real and what isn't. When a celebrity posts a selfie they will obviously only put up the best possible version of themselves.

Any major change will come with consumers refusing to accept brands who use models who are unrealistically young and slim or retouched beyond recognition. Youth should of course be celebrated, but so should other times of life.

Models 1 represents Daphne Selfe, a model in her 80s. Do you see any move towards widening the markers of beauty in fashion?

Daphne is my inspiration: a wonderful lady with fantastic lust for life. There's been some widening of the parameters of different types of beauty, but they remain relatively limited. In the UK, non-Caucasian models are still in the minority but there are more Asian and black models now being used for advertising features – this probably reflects the rise of Asian markets as well as the changing population.

The biggest change has been in the curve model market. More brands are providing clothing in bigger sizes and wanting to use the right girls to promote them. I love seeing these gorgeous ladies' beauty being celebrated. There has been a tendency to called these girls 'plus size', which is negative, so we steer clear of it.

WTF: WHERE'S THE FANTASY?

Ask the fashion industry why they promote such a narrow vision of beauty and you'll get various answers. One of the most common is this: fashion is fantasy, it's not meant to be real life.

Well, ok, let's work with that idea, accepting that catwalks, ads, fashion shoots and red carpets are mainly fantasy. They don't aim (or need) to be representative. We don't watch an awards ceremony and think we should wear a £50,000 dress or a diamond necklace next time we go to the cinema. We don't see a couture editorial and expect our world to be filled with pastel-coloured cats or masque balls in stately homes (more's the pity). These industries produce out-of-the-ordinary ideas and beautiful, dreamy photos – pictures that launch a thousand Pinterest posts.

Hang on though. Fantasy is meant to inspire and uplift, not make you feel like a failure. There's no reason why fantasy couldn't include a bigger range of body shapes and colours. Why not keep the awesome locations and pretty sets and feature women and girls with small waists and large thighs, or broad shoulders and boyish hips or short legs and big boobs? Why are all the models so young? Why not use more models of colour?

Plus, as much as fashion might claim to be fantastical, it's also commercial. There are visionaries focused on creating extraordinary designs or imagery that are their own art forms. Think of the huge, magical and eccentric fairytale productions of fashion photographer Tim Walker, or the late Alexander McQueen's wildly imaginative and perfectly tailored clothes. But fashion is also always big business. Behind the fantasy, those clothes you see on magazine pages have been made to be bought, whether they're a £10,000 coat or a £10 T-shirt. High street stores are just as determined to sell the fantasy of fashion, but make it for the masses. What appears on the catwalks will be available in cheaper forms on the high street within weeks.

What this all boils down to, is that each season's fantasy is actually something chosen by a select group of editors, designers, photographers and stylists – a state of affairs which works out very nicely for the various companies making vast acres of money from those images.

Big businesses tend to play it safe, sticking with what they know works. This means the knock-on message for women is that fantasy only comes in heights between five feet nine and five feet eleven inches. It suggests that every fantasy figure has an extra-slender dress size, a young age and a particular skin tone. Exceptions slip through occasionally, but they are still very much 'the others' – standing apart from established formulas of beauty. It's not much of a fantasy, is it?

Another weapon in the arsenal of fantasy makers is airbrushing. Snow White needs to be completely perfect after all. But it has become less 'mirror, mirror' and more *remove all pores and other signs of life.*

When the general public questions why most fashion image makers retouch all signs that a model or actress might be human, the answer is often unsatisfactory. The usual response from the people protecting their right to retouch, is that we, as a society, need better education on image manipulation. All well and good and useful, but that's not actually a solution to the problem.

What can a bit more awareness about the level to which photos are retouched really do? It's not as simple as saying, 'Look, it exists. Sorry about that. Women don't actually look like that – so stop worrying your pretty little heads about living up to that standard.' We're aware that photo manipulation exists: otherwise we wouldn't be demanding action.

Since photography was discovered, we've been fiddling around with ways to magic away spots and blemishes. The problem now is how easy it is to slim people down or change their complexion in seconds. And that means that pretty much ALL the images we see now are airbrushed. You know what? There is a distinction between a bit of editing for a better shot – tidying up clothes and making a neater image – and a complete reworking of face and body until they resemble a computer-generated idea of a person.

When I model, the resulting photos are recognisably me, but not in the way I'd walk to the shop to buy milk or hang around the house. And it's not just the retouching. Trying to live up to model-me in daily life would require a hairdresser and make-up artist on call, a photographer's assistant to light my skin flatteringly, a personal trainer, and possibly a corset (or at least a good pair of Spanx, for those just-before-a-period days). I'd never get sweaty or have blackheads. My clothes would be crease free. I'd also be a pro at striding around in heels and spontaneously giggling in an attractive way.

It's not just fashion either. All celebrity pictures, whether on catwalks or performing on stage, are carefully selected and photo edited – suggesting that these stars are immaculate all the time. Responding to the singer Lorde's release of an edited photo of herself performing, and one showing her real skin – acne and all – Asima, 17, told me, '*I think Lorde is good because she shows that she's human like us. She's accepting herself and younger girls can look up to someone who has a few spots and isn't perfect.*'

Fantasy is often what attracts us to fashion – the glamour, the gorgeous clothes, the whisper of more imaginative, empowering scenarios. It lifts us temporarily out of our own lives. Yet surely we can have all that fantasy without the hangover that accompanies it?

There are no easy answers to any of this. Retouching isn't going to disappear any time soon, and the industry is slow to make big changes. But what we can do for now is continue to make some noise about issues like ubiquitous retouching or the hyper-narrow view of who can be a model, and all manner of other problems and unfairnesses in the fashion industry. And while we do that, we can also celebrate the brands, designers, photographers, stylists, models, casting directors, magazines, websites and individuals who are doing things a little differently.

THE CHANGING FACE OF FASHION AND BEAUTY

Here's a handful of amazing models who are doing good things to improve diversity in the industry. These women have too many accomplishments to list, so I've focused on their fashion credentials.

- **Aimee Mullins**

  The paralympian and actress had both legs amputated below the knee aged one. In 1999 she appeared in Alexander McQueen's catwalk show wearing wooden prosthetic legs hand-carved with flowers.

- **Naomi Shimada**

  Curve model and presenter Naomi has worked for brands including ASOS, Monki and Free People, and has been a columnist for *Instyle*.

- **Jillian Mercado**

  Jillian is a blogger and fashion editor with muscular dystrophy and has been using a wheelchair since her early teens. In spring 2014 she fronted Diesel's ad campaign.

- **Kelly Knox**

  Born without her left forearm, Kelly first gained exposure in a BBC3 programme called *Britain's Missing Top Model* and has a portfolio of both catwalk and editorial work.

- **Andreja Pejić**

  The face of androgyny in fashion, and model of both menswear and womenswear. In 2014 Andreja came out as transgender, saying that it finally allowed her to be fully comfortable in her body.

- **Chantelle Brown-Young**

  This model, who works under the name Winnie Harlow, has vitiligo – a condition that causes white patches on the skin. She appeared on *America's Next Top Model* and has worked with fashion photographer Nick Knight.

THE PLEASURES AND PITFALLS
OF THE BEAUTY INDUSTRY

Fashion's close cousin is the beauty industry. Here's a business that sells a paradox. Women and teenagers aren't beautiful *enough*, but could be if they only spent more on skin treatments, gym memberships, make-up, hair products, pedicures, fake tan, spa facials, juice cleanses, yoga retreats and chia seeds. Once monetised, beauty becomes something both unreachable and always within sight – and the more money spent, it's hinted, the closer we might get.

This isn't a rant against beauty products or good exercise. I love red lips and mascara-framed eyes and shiny nails and huge amounts of glitter. A good make-up bag is a toolkit, a paint box and a potential source of transformation. Experimenting with changing your looks can be amazing. I'm still awed by the abilities of liquid eyeliner – when I can get it neat enough.

On a more practical level, products such as concealer and cleansers are, if not life-changers, then definitely skin-improvers for those who want to use them – providing a little boost of confidence and an easy way to hide one too many late nights.

Sadly, despite being even closer to the skin of its buyers than the clothing industry, the beauty industry is no better at racial equality. For example, you will usually find that while there are many foundation shades for white skin, there are usually only one or two shades for black skin outside big stores – although lots of newer cosmetic companies are now addressing this, particularly online. This pretty ignorant one-size-fits-all approach is unfair and frustrating. This has direct effects. It makes people feel invisible.

Tara, 16, spoke to me about her Afro hair, describing it as '*a thicket of constantly mutating, gravity-defying, peppercorn-black coils*'. She remembers as a child '*deciding to draw the woman I hoped to become ... a leggy, Caucasian female – complete with blue eyes and a cerise Cupid's bow. Her golden-blonde hair was waist length.*' That was the main image of beauty at hand – an image that's limited at best, damaging at worst.

Tara has now chosen to '*hold on to the ambiguous beauty*' of her appearance, banishing chemical relaxers. But it's still testing in a world where 'Beauty' gets all boxed up and defined in ways that ignore much of the general population.

> *Features in magazines on how to do your hair or your make-up don't work for me. I felt like there was something wrong with me – as though it were my fault I can't find the right foundation!*
>
> Kandace, 19 ◁))

There is nothing wrong with wanting to look good or having pride in your appearance. The key thing behind 'beauty' is that it should be a personal choice to explore and experiment, rather than something that feels like a forced requirement to fit in. Sometimes that's a hard line to tread though. The difference between doing something for personal happiness or to meet other people's expectations is often hard to define.

Do we want to lose weight for ourselves, or because we think we'll be more socially acceptable? Do we slap on foundation because we genuinely enjoy the look of it, or because that's what everyone else does? Usually there isn't an easy answer, but it doesn't mean the questions aren't worth asking.

Although it is perhaps given unnecessary focus, an easy example of that blurred line between personal choice and other people's expectations is body hair. One of the deep-rooted messages, so entrenched that it's often accepted as being normal, is that female body hair is something to be ashamed of. Hairy limbs? Furry bikini line? Take a razor and get to work!

It should be a choice. It's ok if you prefer the look of your legs when smooth. It's also ok if you don't, and want to leave things as they are. The issue is living in a society where, seemingly, the hair from our eyes upwards should be well groomed, but other types of growth should be shaved, waxed or otherwise removed.

For years I disliked vests and sleeveless dresses, worrying that my impossible-to-get-rid-of armpit stubble would be judged by others. Coupled with this was a deeper fear, that if my whole body wasn't as bald as a Barbie, I'd forever remain a virgin. I assumed that all teenage boys would step back in horror at the smallest glimpse of pubic hair. This was backed up by their sniggering references to 'muffs'. A friend's first boyfriend was horrified on realising that she wasn't hairless all over. She reminded him that she wasn't 12, and asked whether he'd be willing to shave his balls. It wasn't a long relationship.

PUBERTY MAKES EVERYTHING WORSE

Body hair is, of course, just one of the pick'n'mix of puberty's delights of spots, sweat, mood swings, extra weight, added height and other body changes. All of these pit stops and pitfalls are by-products of the changes your body goes through while it is slowly, and at times painfully, changing from child into adult.

Puberty begins in primary school for some and nearly the end of secondary school for others. Each of these brings varied trials, especially physically. Start early, and you'll go through changes that it seems like none of your peers understand. In turn, starting puberty late can bring teasing over AA cups and beanpole figures.

Kath, 19, began puberty earlier than her friends, at primary school, and recalls how difficult and disorientating it felt:

I woke up one morning and learned that I could no longer take off my top on a hot day when other girls my age still could. Suddenly there were more areas of my body that had to be covered up. As my thighs grew rapidly and my hips widened, I felt I was inhabiting too much space. I no longer seemed to fit, ashamed of what I felt was my 'fat' body.

I was self-conscious, and getting changed in the classroom under the gaze of boys and the teachers felt uncomfortable. My training bra did nothing to conceal my nipples and I was strangely aware that they were something I needed to hide. When my period started I was angry. It was too soon. I felt afraid of explaining to my primary school teachers just why I could not join in with swimming class. I'd swiftly change my trousers for PE hoping nobody would notice my sanitary towel.

I felt like my boobs, strangely prominent for someone my age, had rudely intruded on my freedom and become something to be ashamed of – even something dangerous that might attract unwanted attention and bullying. I only wish that these concerns had been unwarranted.

I didn't start my periods until I was nearly 15 – and for about a year afterwards they'd come and go without any care for regularity. But my body was still near prepubescent.

There's this continuing assumption that you get that stain in your pants and BAM, everything changes quickly from there. But although it's like that for some, for others puberty is a long and ongoing process.

The female body is complicated. How it's viewed is complicated. How it makes us feel is complicated. And at a point where that body is altering, it's even harder. When you are trying to deal with a nice dose of raging hormones and a physical shape that might be changing unexpectedly, the last thing you need is to be bombarded with messages of what you should look like, feel like and smell like.

In fact, there's often a horrible pong of shame to those messages. For example, as young women, we often seem to be taught that periods are something to keep secret: whether it's smuggling a tampon inside your sleeve so others don't see, or saying you have stomach ache rather than cramps. In many ads for sanitary products blood is transformed into (apparently less offensive?) blue liquid – despite the fact that you'd be booking a doctor's appointment sharpish if you found that in your knickers one morning.

It's framed as shameful. Not just an (often pretty annoying) physical, natural thing. Not just evidence that women are human, that they get sweaty and smelly and yes, some of them bleed (side note: not all women have periods, for a hundred and one different reasons).

It's also worth taking a moment to think about the exciting sides to puberty too. Aside from that whirl and swirl of hormones, it's also a point to start exploring and experimenting – ideally a time of experience, curiosity and change. It can be tough, but there's huge potential for enjoyment, too. And like so many things, it's different for everyone.

The Vagenda: Media Daleks

The Vagenda, run by Rhiannon Lucy Cosslett and Holly Baxter, is a funny, frank and sometimes provocative feminist blog that talks beauty standards, relationships, lads mags and everything in between.

Why did you guys start the Vagenda?

HB: We just felt that magazines weren't representing our lives at all. There wasn't much of an alternative at the time when we started making fun of them, and we wanted to provide a different narrative.

Were you aware of how narrowly focused the media was when you were in your teens?

RLC: I don't think I really had the critical skills to analyse what I was reading. As far as I was concerned, these magazines were the bibles of girlhood. They told me how I should be, what I should be doing. They had all the advice: how to attract boys, what kind of lip-balm to wear while they were kissing you.

What's so damaging about teen magazines?

HB: Those magazines tell you how to all be the same person. Those things start young, the suggestions that you should be a decorative object. Then all your friends try keeping each other in check.

RLC: In that sense women become their own worst enemies, because some start speaking to their friends how magazines talk to their readers, saying, 'Look at her armpit hair', 'ugh, that cellulite'. Girls pick up on that and regurgitate it to their friends.

So was appearance something you were really aware of as teens?

RLC: I hated my body. I hated my freckles. I was a late developer. I remember crying in my mum's arms because I had no tits. It felt like the most important thing a girl could have – and without them, I felt socially doomed forever.

HB: I didn't have boobs at all, but actually found through my teens that I was really distressed at the idea of them. I had a brother the same age and was quite tomboyish. I didn't want to have to be thought of as a woman, didn't want to wear a bra.

RLC: See, I wanted it so much. I even had one of those bras with gel inserts.

HB: To be honest, I was so worried about my face that I wasn't concerned about anything else. I had terrible skin, horrible teeth – I battled against my whole body as a teenager.

What do you think about my comment in this book that on occasion I feel like I should be skinnier - even though, rationally, I know it's ridiculous?

HB: You're always meant to be on that insecurity treadmill, feeling that you're not quite beautiful enough. Even when you criticise that kind of thinking, you can still end up feeling it.

RLC: I still read women's magazines – even though I have a more critical eye, I'll hate-binge on them and feel terrible about myself afterwards. It's like a weird kind of enjoyment in going 'This confirms everything I've been taught.'

HB: I think that's what people found difficult about the Vagenda. The girls who were against it when we went in to schools to talk to them were like, 'Oh you're going to be some holier-than-thou people who aren't affected by women's magazines', and we were like, 'No, that's why we're doing it – because we're SO affected.'

FITNESS FIRST?

It's frustrating that, although both the fashion and beauty industries encourage exercise, it's not in a very healthy way. They suggest your sole motivation should be appearance, not wellbeing (you should look good rather than feel good). That's not to say losing weight can't be a motivation for getting fit, or that you can't feel proud if you do. But it's a balance. The way fitness is presented by the media tends towards a hot body being a trophy rather than anything else. There's less emphasis on treating your body well and looking after it for its own sake. There is also a persistent belief that anything but the skinniest size equals unfit and unhealthy.

It should be much more common to emphasise the importance of health without making value judgements of size. A given body shape is no marker for health and isn't necessarily determined by how well you eat or exercise. Besides, size is no barrier to being a fantastic, gorgeous, graceful athlete. If you just believed the images of sportiness we're fed, you'd assume the epitome of health was incredibly lean. But we're all built differently. People run marathons or regularly swim or dance ballet or are just really, really fit and still wear a bigger dress size. To assume that large automatically means unhealthy is to have a blatant lack of knowledge about body types.

Skinny-shaming and fat-shaming both happen far too often (once is too often). Each is as bad as the other, but the latter is more widespread. It's so damaging that some girls and women are terrified of publishing a photo of themselves online, or asking for help while trying clothes on.

However, what connects the shamed is that the shamers assume – and accuse in loud voices – that the people they are attacking *must be* eating the wrong things. Do you know what? It doesn't matter if people are over- or underweight because that is the natural way they look, or because they are having a tough time and not quite looking after themselves properly. Why should some people's size allow complete strangers to make catty, downright rude comments? Body size is not something others have a right to criticise or be bitchy about. Skinny-shaming, fat-shaming, whatever it is – it's time to stop judging and instead focus on appreciating our own marvellous bodies.

The way people eat and exercise and the way they look is not always a straightforward equation. Some people can seem to eat what they like and remain slender while others make careful nutritional choices and still put on weight (particularly in their teens). Body size is determined by so many things: genetics, rate of metabolism and much more. In the world we live in, we are surrounded by constant pressure to be thin and conflicting advice about what we should or should not be eating: it's bewildering. We think we are doing the right thing, and then a few weeks later that same advice is called into question. Foods and products and diets are championed and demonised faster than we can keep up with – one minute eating too much fat is bad for you, then salt, then sugar.

The truth about our obsession with some kind of 'perfect' figure is that we actually live in a society where the general population's average size is growing larger. Despite the range of sugar-free or fat-free – and sometimes any-kind-of-real-food-free – products being touted, too many people are edging towards serious weight gain and obesity, particularly children too young to do anything about it.

Never before has there been so much cheap, ready-made food available to provide a quick spike in energy. This is generally food packed full of hidden fats and sugars and all kinds of other gross stuff that isn't good for you. Couple this with an almost complete lack of education on how to make nutritious meals cheaply, the massive problem of food affordability, and the fact cake tastes bloody amazing, and you get a recipe for disaster – but we're all still chowing down.

Much like my complaint that no one seems to be able to take a balanced view of the modelling industry, start talking about weight and you quickly unpack a general sense of collective panic and confusion. I guess that it's partly down to the fact that quiet talk about doing a bit of exercise and eating quite healthy foods won't help shift any one of a million diet products or deliver eye-catching editorials.

It doesn't help that exercise isn't usually actively encouraged for girls, even though it's about the best possible thing for physical and mental health. How often do we hear about the simple fun of keeping fit and enjoying what your body can do?

I have a love/hate relationship with exercise. I go through phases of adoring jogging or feeling indescribably content after a really long hike. These moments are rare though. In between these bursts of activity there are months where I feel genuinely guilty for my inactivity – usually because I'll prioritise other things (like binge-watching Netflix shows), or just can't face the idea. At uni I cycle everywhere, which is a clever way to slip exercise into the day without thinking about it.

For everything else though, I have to try and consider it like one of my favourite occasional pastimes, wild swimming. For me, doing exercise is a bit like plunging into a cold river. Wild swimming is something I really, really look forward to, but at the same time, taking the leap is hard, and cold ... and frequently muddy. Buuuuut once you are in it's great, and there's the glowing feeling when you do it and are out and dry again.

Hopefully the way we all think about exercising is changing, if slowly, especially as female teams and sportswomen get better media coverage, and ace initiatives like This Girl Can, are making strides in the right direction. But it has to become more acceptable for women to be sweaty and smelly and strong – to work out or go running or swim or play football or whatever else because it's fun and satisfying to push yourself rather than because it has any bearing on how attractive you're seen to be.

MIRROR, MIRROR?

I like beauty with multiple meanings and possibilities: inner, outer, unconventional, individual. Beauty can be incredibly positive, but only when it's celebrated in all its forms.

We all appreciate beauty on some level. Most of us get a thrill from knowing that someone else likes our looks. Whether it's the confidence in a fabulous skirt or being told that you're gorgeous, that heady knowledge that you're appreciated can be wonderful.

It gets trickier when self-worth is based solely on others' responses. In an ideal world, being told you're beautiful or amazing or compelling would be a boost, but you wouldn't need it. You'd already know that you were beautiful and amazing and compelling. This would just be a fun little plus, a sparked sense of satisfaction. Yet a lot of young people don't believe that they have these qualities unless the message is reinforced by those around them.

> *I've grown to realise that charisma makes up for any kind of appearance.*
>
> Dina, 19

It's tough when girls are actively encouraged to be beautiful more than brilliantly brainy; when girls are told that their worth is tied up with how they look or how they present themselves to the world rather than in quiet virtues like being a thoughtful person who's always interested in others.

It's not just a problem that affects women, although women and girls have borne the brunt of this kind of thinking for much longer. There are massive rising pressures on men and boys too. Whether it's competition in the gym, clothes choices, careful diets, emphasis on abs maintenance or grooming products, the pressure to look a particular way isn't just the preserve of the female half of the population.

Yet it remains true that women, in particular, become their bodies: gossip magazines criticising some star's yo-yo dieting, online tabloids using creepy 'all grown up' captions for famous young women just turned 16, prominent women getting tweet after tweet telling them that they're ugly, fashion magazines delivering a constant stream of celebrity skincare secrets and workout routines (as if that defines those women's achievements), the endless carefully considered selfie snaps, iPhone held aloft and flat stomach on display.

To an extent we are our bodies. We are our ability to choose what we do with them: dress them up, feed them, nurture them. They allow us to dance, walk, play football, lift heavy things, have sex, control a wheelchair, cycle, hold someone else close, run for the bus, be an acrobat (if you're ambitious), and maybe even have children if we want them. But we are much more than the sum total of our bodies – we are so much more than how we look.

And yes, your body image *is* important. But it's not important in the way society or bitching at school makes it out to be. Importance isn't measured in popularity or dress size. It's marked by how you see yourself. It's marked in having confidence in your own body, in viewing it as something marvellous and amazing rather than being the potential evidence of lack or failure.

Regardless of size, I always aim to fill up the space that I stand in, and make it mine. I want to be strong and stride, and never apologise for my height or my shape. I like having presence, to dress as I want and for people to know when I walk into a room.

IS FEMINISM THE ANSWER?

The first thing I remember about discovering feminism is the thrill of the word itself. At age 15 or 16, it suddenly began popping up in all the books, blogs, articles and tweets I was reading. It was a word I could apply to everything from feeling frustrated about the image of women I saw in the media to the fact I was told it was more dangerous for me, being female, to walk down a street by myself at night. There was no single use, no one thing it stood for – other than, at its most basic core, the need for gender equality. Political, social and economic equality, if you want to get technical (which I always do).

Kate Nash: The Musician

Kate is a Platinum-selling singer-songwriter and actress. Outspoken in her views on feminism, she's long been supportive of young women.

What does the word 'feminism' mean to you?

It's believing that men and women are equal, that all humans deserve a right to a happy, safe and fulfilling life.

Can anyone be a feminist?

Anyone, female or male who believes in equality for both sexes is a feminist. Anyone who has a platform to speak on has a responsibility to talk about what they believe in.

Do you think it's important for women in the media to talk about feminism?

There are so many global examples of women being sidelined, abused, denied education, violated – so yes, I think it is extremely important for women, especially women in the media and women of influence, to discuss the issues.

Why do you think feminism isn't shouted about more often?

Feminism really isn't a dirty word, even though it often carries that stigma. I've learned to appreciate that feminism means something different to everyone. And I think that's key. There'll never be a unified agreement on any ideology because we're all far too different. Feminism is about empowering women – and all women are complex creatures with different lives, needs and desires.

Is it difficult being a woman in the public eye?

I've definitely had some bad experiences in music! I'm sure every girl has. I've been the target of a lot of aggression and sexist remarks from guys in the crowd. It was difficult at first, but I just carried on playing and stood up for myself. Those kind of defining performances are important for female artists.

Do you think the music industry is sexist?

The music industry is still pretty sexist and there is still a lack of female artists. I'm always campaigning for more girls to get into music. It is exciting to see a lot of all-girl bands coming out like Vulkano, Charli XCX, La Sera, Peach Kelli Pop, The Tuts, Haim, Skating for Polly and Dum Dum Girls. It definitely feels like there is a shift underway, but there is still a lot of work to do.

How do you think the change will come about?

The great thing is that this generation of girls will inspire the next and it will keep growing and we will keep fighting sexism. Girls need to keep breaking boundaries, not taking 'no' for an answer and being brave. Women are growing and changing and being challenged constantly. It's exciting.

Why did you set up the Rock'n'Roll for Girls After School Music Club?

I was extremely frustrated with what I was being presented with at the time. It was 2010 – everyone was making a huge fuss over 'how many women' were in the music industry. Yet there was still predominantly coverage of male musicians in media and male line-ups at festivals. I went to speak on a panel about the gender gap in the music industry and was shocked at how bad our situation really was.

What's the aim of your work?

I want more female musicians, more female songwriters. I want the idea of a female musician to be less of a shock. So that's why I started the clubs, to initiate change in young girls' minds, give them the confidence to believe in themselves and awareness that music is an option for all girls and women no matter what you're told.

F- YOU? F- ME TOO

For me, the F word stands for a desire to see more women in positions of power and authority. It stands for fighting back against all those who think they need to worry about women being too sexual or not sexual enough. It stands for wanting to see the wage gap closed: equal pay for equal work. It stands for looking at how racism interacts with sexism. It stands for changing attitudes around the phrase 'asking for it'. It stands for asking hundreds and hundreds of questions on everything from domestic violence to fashion advertising. For me, it's a toolkit. No single use. Lots of possibilities.

It's also a set of tools you can learn to wield with more skill over time – like the movement itself, you can always learn, expand and improve. For example, in more recent years I have begun to understand that the absolute best thing about feminism is that it's not just about me. What makes us human is partly our ability to engage with other people's stories. I'm all for recognising the limits of our own experiences, and looking outward to the vast range of everyone else's. That's why plenty of the feminist things I want to write and campaign and shout about haven't necessarily happened to me. Caring about equality isn't just about caring for your *own* state of equality, but that of everyone else too.

Feminism has uses beyond empowering girls and women, too. It also means encouraging boys and men to escape the boundaries placed on them by society, especially when it comes to stupid stereotypes and expectations. It means obliterating phrases like 'man up' and making sure that anyone can feel free to cry or to talk about their feelings. It means that men can be stay-at-home parents without being questioned. It means less limitation of life choices, and fighting for all sorts of brilliant types of equality that will ultimately benefit EVERYONE.

Of course, feminism is a very personal thing. When I was 16, I wrote about feminism giving me a choice and a voice. I still believe that. My personal feminism involves dressing exactly as I please, speaking up on all sorts of things (and very happily arguing back), never assuming that my gender should hold me back in my work, talking and writing about a range of things from body image to sexuality, calling out stuff that's dodgily sexist, and generally being ever so independent – and STILL getting pissed off at the whole not-going-around-by-myself-in-the-dark thing. But I know that the word and the movement mean different things to different people.

Learning about feminism involves a lot of listening to and respecting other women's choices, hearing their voices and where they are coming from, acknowledging exactly why equality is important to them, and in what specific ways. One of the more wonderful things we can thank the internet for is the sheer number of voices you can find there, especially when feminist zines, websites, blogs and vlogs are springing up everywhere. So many of these have been started up by young people. There is passion and drive – and anger – aplenty.

FINDING
YOUR STYLE

2

WHAT IS STYLE?

There was a funny phrase I heard a lot at first when I became a model: 'I like your look.' This fashion-speak was directed at my outfits – not my face. It was noted when I was scouted, the agent nodding at my knitted minidress and big earrings. It happened again on my first ever shoot. The stylist mentioned that part of their reason for choosing me was the vintage bolero top I'd been wearing in my portfolio pictures – it had full sleeves, a row of buttons and lace trim.

I heard the phrase again on one of the only days of castings I ever did. I was sent along to (among others) Burberry's headquarters wearing a tiny, mint-green, 1960s tunic with buckles up the front (I'd bought it from a vintage shop called Beyond Retro) – and some staggeringly tall grey lace-up boots. They liked my look, too – although not enough to book me.

I hadn't always dressed like that. From the ages of 10 to 13 I mainly lived in diamanté-encrusted hoodies, slogan T-shirts, baker boy hats, cartoon-print tops and trainers. I discarded the neon colours and cargo trousers in Year Eight, replacing them with charity shop finds and plenty of old stuff snaffled from my mum's wardrobe – stuff that we were just learning to call vintage.

I still love clothing, to the point that my wardrobe is so full I can't close the door properly. There's a joy in putting together a good outfit. Delving into my wardrobe for new treasures and combinations is a game I still enjoy every morning.

When I'm wearing an outfit that I like, it makes me feel good – better than that, fabulous – setting me up for whatever the day ahead might bring. Whether it's a killer pair of shorts, a crisp silk shirt or a long dress that allows me to waft around in a vaguely artsy way, the right combination boosts my mood and confidence.

Choosing how to present yourself is not the only way to use clothing, for some it becomes more like armour. As much as clothes are a way to 'express yourself', an outfit can change or conceal, as well as reveal, personality.

THE NECESSARY EVIL OF SCHOOL UNIFORMS

The vast majority of young people spend five days a week in school uniform, in styles ranging from the regulation hideous to the just about acceptable. In my final two years, I took to wearing brogues to retain a tiny bit of individuality. I found some men's ones in a charity shop. They were made of stiff leather and I wore them until they fell apart. I hated the rest of the uniform. The day I left school, I took a pair of nail scissors to my jumper, snipping it into ribbons. Getting to sixth form and wearing my own clothes every day was kind of momentous.

There are advantages to the uniform though. It gives regularity and helps break down barriers between different upbringings and social status. Bea, 14, observed that, *'I don't like wearing school uniform, but I do really think it helps to bring down social divisions.'* The school uniform can't do away completely with our natural urge to stand out or showcase our personalities though, and other things such as bags or shoes tend to become status symbols instead. So uniforms may not be perfect – but when your mind is filled with so many other things, sometimes it's pretty useful not having to stress about a full new outfit each morning.

WHY I STARTED A STYLE BLOG

When I was 14, I started my blog, Clothes, Cameras and Coffee. Style blogging was still quite a new idea, and one that the fashion industry was just picking up on. A lucky few bloggers began getting front row seats at catwalk shows, and street-style 'what are they wearing' photography hit the mainstream. I, like plenty of girls sitting in their bedrooms all over the world, said 'I want to do that too!'

At that time my own life was a strange mix of innocence, excitement and unhappiness. I struggled socially, but was kept happy by other worlds: books, style, film and photography. I watched classic movies like *The Red Shoes* and *Breakfast at Tiffany's*, read *The Bell Jar* and started listening to some of my parents' old music. Thanks to my modelling trips, I also discovered the vintage delights of Brick Lane in London.

The previous year, my friend Flo and I began doing photography shoots together. These usually involved a loose theme, things from my wardrobe flung into a bag, and a day spent somewhere with a camera. They grew more elaborate over the years – the locations wilder, the stories stronger, the clothes increasingly outrageous – but all had their roots in the same place. It was about getting together, having fun, throwing around ideas, chatting and giggling more than serious working.

What was (and is) so lovely about our photography adventures is how they continue something we first explored together as children, when we'd spend afternoons emptying out the dressing-up box. There's a snap of us, joined by Flo's older sister: a trio in big-brimmed hats and wearing heels three times too big, lipstick smeared across our mouths and our shoulders wrapped in sparkly scarves. All this fed into our later projects: the dressing-up box raided once more.

As the blog grew, I began experimenting outside of the shoots with my mum's own student-purchased 1950s skirts and vintage jackets. She had two clear plastic boxes hidden in the back of a cupboard, each filled with tissue-paper-wrapped things from jumble sales or late great-aunts that she'd kept since her teens and 20s. They're still there now, but the boxes are nearly empty. Most of the contents are in my room.

SOME HANDY TIPS FOR BLOG SHOOTS 〰️➡️

Here is what I picked up hunting around for the perfect photography spot.

✱ Don't be afraid of spontaneity. Some of my best shoots were when an unexpected visit from a friend turned into an extended wardrobe raid.

✱ If it is pre-planned, think about working up a narrative or theme in advance. Flo and I did one shoot inspired by the author Angela Carter's dark reworkings of fairytales, another responding to lots of myths and stories from the sea. For shoots with other photographers or models, I'd often make collages outlining my ideas, or we'd construct a specific character for them to play – fairy queens of the countryside or *Alice in Wonderland* imagined in every era from the 1950s to the 1980s.

✱ Scrapbooks can be useful for sparking ideas: rip things out of newspapers and magazines, pick up arts leaflets, juxtapose unexpected photos, stick in fabrics or book pages and add your own sketches. They're great for flicking back through if you seem to have run out of concepts.

✱ Be a magpie – keep an eye out for outlandish items to dress up in sometime in the future. 1970s wedding gowns? Capes? Cheap faux pearls that can be layered up? Lengths of Liberty fabric? Sometimes things that look extremely odd on the hanger can be transformed when worn. Build up a collection of belts and scarves too.

✱ Make sure you have a supply of safety pins and bulldog clips. These can reshape the look of an item of clothing viewed from the front – it doesn't matter what's bunched, tucked, tied, clipped and pinned at the back.

Think about how outfits interact with location. I once picked up a shiny green dress I would never usually wear (£1 from a charity shop sale rail) that suddenly looked amazing when Flo wore it knee-deep in seawater at 8am on a summer's morning.

 Check the weather forecast if you're going to be outside. Rain ruins plans (although I did once do a whole set of photos with a friend jumping through puddles and swinging her umbrella with gleeful abandon). Also, don't leave it until too late in the day. In one particularly memorable *Snow White and Rose Red* influenced shoot, Flo and I spent so long getting ready that by the time we'd driven up a winding track and hiked over several fields to reach the woods, it was nearly dark …

 Obviously urban and rural settings have their own plus and minus points, but whether you're surrounded by hills or buildings, keep an eye out for anything that's going to make an interesting backdrop. And there's no harm in asking permission for most locations. Really polite requests can go a long way.

With a blog to supply I could search eBay and flea markets in the hunt for hidden treasures, or have a reason to get excited at discovering all my great-grandma's hats. There was something pushing me to put together fantastical outfits to tramp around forests and jump into lake-sized puddles.

I was lucky to begin style blogging when I did. The internet was a much smaller world back then. I experienced it first as a hobby, and did it for the love of clothing and the joy of making newfound connections with like-minded people, from other teens through to women in their 40s and beyond. It was a diverse bunch, not only in age, but their lifestyles and backgrounds too. I followed bloggers from America, from Sweden, from South Africa, from France, from Japan – and gained good friends closer to home. The sense of community and opportunity was so fresh.

More than six years on and my blog is still going. Where once I used it to escape beyond my small village, now it's another way to be creative. It's become somewhere to pick apart ideas and comment on fashion, books or whatever else takes my fancy. What remains the same though is the delight of putting a post together, clicking 'publish' and having no idea who might end up reading it, or responding.

STARTING A BLOG ⅏➔

With everyone and their third cousin having started a blog at one time or another, I don't have many new top tips to add. The two most important parts for me are community and conversation.

✱ Find blogs that inspire you. Comment on them and say why you get excited when you click on their page. Is it fabulous photos? Articles that get you thinking? Belly-laugh humour? Don't just go for ones with thousands of readers.

✱ Consider what subjects get you going. What do you want to talk about? What kinds of conversations do you want to set alight?

Work on your content before you post it. If it's writing, then practise as much as you can. Read it aloud. Remove any sentences that don't need to be there. Ask for feedback. Polish it more. Accept that it's a gradual skill to build up over time.

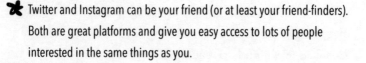 Read! Get aware of what's going on out there in the world. Seek out essays by amazing writers, familiarise yourself with all sorts of fiction, assess what you like and don't like. Look to the past, as well as what's happening now.

Twitter and Instagram can be your friend (or at least your friend-finders). Both are great platforms and give you easy access to lots of people interested in the same things as you.

Be responsive. If you read a brilliant article or blog post – tell that person how much you enjoyed it. We tend to focus on the nastiness that gets thrown around the internet, but it's worth letting other people know when their words meant something very special.

Remain receptive to other opinions. Debates allow you to see all sorts of perspectives, and even strengthen your own position. I realised I cared much more about ethical fashion when I had to defend it.

Eleanor Hardwick: Teen Photographer

Eleanor Hardwick is a photographer and curator with an impressive CV, having worked for *Rookie* magazine, Vogue.com, and Urban Outfitters.

How did you first get involved with photography?

I started taking pictures when I was 12, uploading them to Flickr. It was simply an extension of what I had always done; as a child I was constantly making zines, designing houses, doodling all over my school books, sewing, making short films.

Was starting young in the industry an advantage or a drawback?

My age allowed me to stand out from the others I suppose, and I feel like creating work about yourself is key. There are so many middle-aged white men creating work about young girls that just seems irrelevant to me. On the other side, people have tried to take advantage of me many times. You have to stay strong and not let yourself be manipulated by people older than you.

Why have you focused so much on teen girls in your work?

Adolescence is a very confusing time because it's a limbo between being a child and adult. To a lot of teenagers that can be very surreal and it's easy to get lost on the way to finding yourself. It's even harder as a girl. I try to convey this in my pictures: the serendipity of youth and the feeling of making it up as you go along.

Do you think your work is a reflection of how you felt as a teen?

I was once told that the best artists create work about what they know best. It always seemed natural to treat my artistic expression as autobiographical, instead of trying to tell someone else's story.

FITTING IN VS. STANDING OUT

When it comes to what you wear and how you want to present yourself, this is the big debate. What's your goal with style? Do you want to melt into the crowd? Wear whatever you want to? Have a uniform? Go for what everyone else is buying? Are you determined to own a huge, sprawling wardrobe? Would you rather not have to think about clothes at all?

Your clothes choices don't happen in isolation. As well as saying something about your personality, they suggest how you relate to those around you. Are you happiest wearing the same kind of gear as your friends or do you feel more comfortable when you are being creative around the edges of current trends?

There's this assumption with teens that everyone wants to blend in. It's true with some people, but there are loads more who are happy to go their own way, and plenty more who'd love to – but are a bit afraid of what others might say. We've all been there: that's when the 'what to wear' issue causes more anxiety than it should do, when decisions over outfits become interwoven and weighed down with status, popularity, judgement and identity. What a nightmare.

My personal style is inspired by all kinds of influences and fuelled by charity shop discoveries. This started in my early teens, but although I was entirely comfortable with my vintage pleated skirts, patterned maxi-dresses and big cardigans at home, I worried they'd mark me too far apart from everyone else. On No Uniform days at school I wore T-shirts, leaving grandma's blouses in my wardrobe. I didn't want to draw too much attention to myself.

Despite being happily individual at home or among friends elsewhere, the pressure to be like everyone else at school held strong sway. I felt like I needed to blend in, but I never quite could. At least I had a blog where I could let it all loose, and wear and write about clothes that made me confident, rather than ones that helped me blend in with everyone else.

I don't really like being a sheep. It's boring. But it's so easy to fall into the trap of dressing or behaving like everyone else, because it's expected.

Jemima, 16

When I began at sixth form I thought I'd remain faithful to my style – but water it down. I'd wear my silk shirts and loafers, but with jeans instead. Well, that lasted all of about two weeks. Then I chucked all caution away and decided to wear whatever I liked. By the second year, I was known (mostly positively) for how I dressed.

What I learned moving from fitting in to standing out a bit more was twofold. 1) People grow up. They stop caring as much about what others wear and they get over the pettiness. 2) I had nothing to be ashamed of, and in fact, people respected my choices.

I think with teens, style choices can become intermingled with a horrible popularity game too many people play. On-trend clothing can become sought after because we know it will bring admiration. Whether it's affording an expensive handbag, or owning a particular branded jumper, it suggests that you have the same cash or social credit as everyone else.

Whenever I got a new haircut or a bag, I wanted compliments from friends. I'd envy them and in turn want them to envy me.

Helen, 19

WHERE DOES CONFIDENCE COME FROM?

One afternoon, I bumped into someone from my sixth form in a vintage shop. We knew each other by sight from the train we caught each morning from different stops, and so we introduced ourselves. After chatting for a while she pointed out a stunning dress and said, 'I'd love to wear that, but I'd be afraid of getting judged.'

I've never forgotten that tiny encounter because it put my own fears in perspective, and made me realise that I had gradually managed to defeat my wardrobe demons. Having your clothing choices dictated by fear of what others might think is exhausting – a game of guesswork in which others' disapproval becomes the awful end-consequence, to be avoided at all costs.

We are told over and over that other people's opinions don't matter. But it's soooo much easier to *say* that than act on it. I care about what other people think, try as I might to tell myself I don't. Unfortunately you can't wave a pair of vintage Yves Saint Laurent shoes at your wardrobe and expect your worries to vanish overnight. But we *can* do our best to choose the degree to which we let others' opinions affect us.

There are tons of quotes shared online in a vaguely 'let's-be-all-inspirational-and-meaningful-with-pretty-fonts-and-pictures-of-a-sunset' kind of way, to the tune of Eleanor Roosevelt's famous statement that 'No one can make you feel inferior without your consent.' Another favourite of mine (but please hold the sunset) is, 'What other people think of me is none of my business.'

Both these quotes promote the idea that others' comments should have no impact – that we should care little what anyone else thinks of us, and have the presence of mind to retain our choice in the matter. But as easy as it is to let an inspirational statement trip off the tongue, it can be harder to act on it.

What these quotes actually suggest to me is a reclaiming of power. They're talking about that very real need to realise that living your life afraid of others' opinions is a waste. It's ok to feel hurt by others' words or actions. It's ok if you're not the strongest, most super-confident 'I'm not taking any of your bollocks' kind of person. But that shouldn't mean choosing your clothes becomes dictated by other people: we can look for tools and tricks to care a little bit less about what other people think.

Is there a specific formula that whisks away all fears? If there is, please write and tell me (wait? What am I saying? Tweet! It's quicker), because I haven't found it. But there are some small practical things that will help. First, fake it. Sometimes you have to go through the motions and act stuff out – even if beneath you're a gibbering, nervous wreck. Doing whatever leaves you afraid, whether that's wearing what *you want to* rather than what's expected or leaving the house without make-up or turning up to a party with unashamedly hairy armpits, can be super-liberating. Often the anticipation is worse than any actual response.

I don't dress up for other people, but because it makes me feel better about myself. Other people aren't living their lives to please you, so why should you try to please them?

Asima, 17 📢

Plus, think about what this is going to do for your attitude. Often you command more respect through suggesting in behaviour and body language that you respect yourself, and have nothing to apologise for. It's all in looking (even if you're not feeling) confident, secure and at ease with who you are. If you project a sense of feeling happy about how you look then others are going to have a harder job trying to put you down.

Obviously it's one of those big 'easier said than done' things – the kind that's simple to preach from the other side. I stuck it out for a while before it worked, but work it did. These days, I'm likely to be found striding around in all sorts of wonderful, ridiculous things (ankle-length leather coats? Bright orange pleated sixties trapeze dresses? Blue velvet blazers with matching boots? Yes pleeeaaaase!). I wear them because they give me joy – and I can't imagine letting anyone else stand in the way of that.

✦

ADVICE ON YOUR NEW LOOK

Sometimes when you're nervous about a particular style choice (or anything else, for that matter), it's worth thinking things through in advance.

 What's the worst that could possibly happen? Often we're not quite sure exactly what we're afraid of. If that worst possible thing is someone else's opinion, unravel it further. Why does this person's judgement matter? Who does it say more about – me, or the person small-minded enough to judge?

 If anyone did say anything, how would you respond? Thinking up answers in advance can be reassuring, even if you don't need to use them.

 Where does this anxiety come from? Friends? Family? The unspoken codes of school? And will any of them give a damn if you do things your own way instead?

 Will this matter to you in one month, six months, a year, five years, a decade? Is it possible that these shoes just seem like a big deal right at this very exact moment, but won't even be remembered in the future?

A SMALL NOTE ON WHAT YOUR CLOTHES DON'T SAY

When it comes to clothes, there are some messages that outfits *don't* give out – never have, never will. It's incredible to me that some people seem to think that girls who show off their bodies are worth less than their covered-up counterparts. It's a crappy social judgement. Imagine flipping the image – or, rather, flipping the gender balance. What would your response or reaction be if you overheard a conversation like this between two women?

> 'Did you hear about that guy who *reckons* he got assaulted by a girl he knew?'
> 'Yeah! I've seen that guy. He's always cycling around wearing those tight shorts.'
> 'I know, right? Gorgeous bum, and those abs! Bloody poser though – always getting them out.'
> 'You can hardly blame a girl for staring when it's that blatant. If you show off those kinds of muscles, you've gotta accept the consequences. What does he expect?'
> 'After all, women just can't help themselves when there's that much on display.'
> 'God, I wonder what he was wearing when he got attacked? Bet it was one of those skin-tight vests.'

'I don't get it. Guys like him could just cover it up a bit: No need for those shorts outlining everything. It's like he secretly wanted it to happen.'

I felt slightly uncomfortable even writing that. It's just as bad as the relentless discussions about what women wear – the difference being that this exchange is ridiculous because it would never happen. With guys, there's no question an outfit could be the *cause* of anything. It'd be great if we could make that standard, regardless of gender. There is no particular scoop of a top that says you're 'asking for it' or a point above the knee where skirts move from acceptable to accountable. Clothing says absolutely, entirely bugger all about consent.

SUPER SEWING FOR LAZY DAYS

When I began my blog, I wanted nothing more than to become a fashion designer. I'd spend hours drawing out ideas, yet I usually faltered before reaching the sewing machine. On the page I could imagine a ball gown threaded together with spiders' webs; in reality anything beyond very basic sewing skills scared me. I realised that I was better suited to writing lines of text than straightening the lines of a seam.

I didn't come away from my fashion designer dreams empty-handed though, I did gain a limited but exceptionally useful understanding of some short-cut delights to new outfits. My mum first showed me the art of lazy alteration and the rules are simple: do everything with the minimum of time and effort for the maximum change and impact. These are hardly the skills of a trained professional seamstress but they've always served me well.

Pins and decent scissors are vital. Tailor's chalk is helpful for marking new hems but you can get by with washable water-based felt tips or even a soft pencil. You'll need a ruler or tape measure if you want a little more accuracy than my usual 'oh I'll just do it by eye' thinking. You don't even need a sewing machine for basic work: all you need is a needle and thread. Are you ready?

Dress in need of a closer fit?

You can simply turn the dress inside out and pin the side seams tighter, before sewing into place and trimming the new seams. OR you can do an even-easier thing with two lengths of ribbon in a vaguely matching colour and a needle and thread.

Put on the dress and pin a length of ribbon onto each side seam at the waist, or slightly higher than the waist if you prefer. Tie loosely at the back to see how well the ribbons pull in the front of the dress – you should have a much better fit. If you're happy with the way the fabric now gathers at the back, sew the ribbons in place, and voilà!

Too long?

Whether it's a skirt, dress or trousers, cutting and turning a new hem is your most useful skill. Having said that, it's one of those things that feels like it ought to be faster to do than it is.

The simple solution is to hack off 30cm from the bottom of a dress and wear it as is – and I must admit, occasionally that's exactly what I do. However, the slightly-more-effort way to shorten a hem is always worth it if you are serious about making over your clothes; look it up!

Want to turn your trousers into shorts?
Everyone knows you can make denim cut-off shorts by using a pair of scissors to attack a pair of jeans. With the patience to add hems, you can create as many pairs of velvet shorts as you could possibly need. I made my collection by buying velvet trousers from charity shops, lopping off the legs and sewing new hems.

Save the best till last
There are tons of sewing tutorials online that can show you all this in practice. The secret is to start with a few garments you were never that sure about or keen on before you try this on any favourites.

WHO ARE YOU WEARING?

It's well established that clothes are staggeringly wonderful in their ability to transform appearance. Between a well-stocked wardrobe and a dressing table there are thousands of characters, looks and get-ups out there. And yet, those wonderful possibilities depend on an industry that relies on cheap labour, horrendous working conditions and some pretty dodgy practices in order to produce those nice new dresses (and make lots of profit).

So, humour me. Take a second to cast an eye over what you're wearing. Any idea whose hands pieced together the material and stitched it? Unless a rather lovely family member or friend made it, the answer is probably, 'I have no idea' (as it would be for me too). And that's ok. It'd be impossible to name, or know much, about anyone who made most of the stuff we own – whether it's clothes, ready meals, or cushions. We consume things all the time without weighing up who produced them.

What about where in the world was it made? Again, without taking our clothes off and turning them inside out, most of us can't answer that straight off. With a few exceptions, every item of clothing has had some journey from fibres to fabric to factories to shop floors. It's a journey we rarely consider.

A while back I realised I was increasingly uncomfortable with my lack of knowledge. Who'd stitched the collar of my favourite top? How old was the individual who'd delicately sewn those buttons in place? Around the time that these questions surfaced, I discovered Lucy Siegle's book, *To Die For: Is Fast Fashion Wearing Out the World?* I'd been sent it to review for my blog, but it turned out to have a huge impact on how I shopped.

Siegle uses the term fast fashion to describe the way we buy clothes – how we are encouraged to see them as cheap, expendable, easy to throw out and replace with something new. The rate at which new clothes are churned out is faster than it's ever been before. Shop stock changes regularly to encourage you to buy it today in case it's gone next week. Trends seen on the catwalks are replicated as quickly as possible on the high street. No pauses, just a relentless ebb and flow of clothes. There are three things in particular she mentioned that I now try to remain mindful of, and read up on whenever I can before buying clothes.

1) Treatment of workers

Often people making clothes are paid very little (in *To Die For*, Lucy Siegle gave the figure of 1.5p for a £4 T-shirt). They're at the bottom of the supply chain, sometimes barely earning enough to survive. Ridiculous working hours, child labour, mistreatment of employees, banning trade unions, inadequate facilities, no sick leave or maternity rights … listing all the various issues in detail could form a chapter of its own. Lots of work environments aren't safe to spend each very long day in, or are deadly: read up on the Rana Plaza building collapse in

Bangladesh, as well as the Tazreen factory fire that killed more than 100 people.

2) Impact on environment

Clothes production can do serious damage, especially to things like water supply, both in using it up (cotton is a water-guzzling plant, according to the WWF it takes up to 2,700 litres to create enough to make a single T-shirt), and polluting it (dye and chemicals used on textiles often do awful, awful things to water supplies). Creating clothes at the pace and volume we now expect dominates resources that are needed for other things, like ... drinking.

3) Our throwaway culture

We are encouraged to buy, buy, buy more and more – to never be satisfied, always questing for the new, the updated, the better. That means we chuck more and more too. We have become convinced that if we just buy that one extra dress or this fantastic new skirt then we will be happier, more attractive, lead a better life. You know what? Feeling unhappy with everything you currently own won't help anything – and neither will sinking all your money on the next big trend. Voracious shopping sprees and binning last year's acquisitions to make way for more stuff you don't need isn't happiness: it's a recipe for dissatisfaction.

Part of the issue is that high street stores have really long, complicated supply chains – with orders for new clothes passed through lots of different hands before they actually end up being made in a particular factory. This allows those stores to hold up their hands and go: 'AAAH, we didn't know! Nothing to do with us! Had no idea people were being treated awfully to make our crop tops super-cheap. Sorrynotsorry', when they're caught out.

My own response is to avoid the high street as much as possible, apart from necessities like socks and bras – I can't quite afford British-made gorgeous lingerie. I also buy a lot of vintage and second-hand clothes, and try to support more sustainable and independent designers when possible. Although these clothes can be more expensive, I'll save up and buy one or two beautiful new things every now and then, valuing their presence in my wardrobe all the more because I know I'll wear them for a long time to come; savouring the process of deliberating, thinking, imagining and finally making my decision.

> *It would feel so wrong to endorse fast fashion ever again, and it makes you feel so good to support companies that are doing the right thing – a single purchase can make a big difference.*
>
> Willow, 15 🔊

There are also still plenty of mainstream labels I (occasionally) drool over too – I'm really not shrugging on a nettle waistcoat here. I'm also not claiming that I'm perfect, I've bitten my lip before on seeing a 'made in China' label on a new pair of velvet boots. I'm also very aware that I'm typing these words on a laptop that was probably made in horrendous conditions, and has components made out of minerals that are mined in unethical ways.

Living a life completely free of harming others through what we buy would require living in a wood hut with a vegetable patch and some hand-reared chickens. But that doesn't stop me trying to make active choices as and when I can. Some awareness and small changes in your buying habits are better than none at all. I began making small steps towards ethical, sustainable fashion by looking at the contents of my own wardrobe. I make better distinctions than I used to between clothes that help solve the problem of unethical fashion, and those that harm people, or our environment, directly.

TOP CHARITY SHOP TIPS *Mmm→*

One of the best ways I found to change my shopping habits was to start sourcing more things second hand. This isn't a long-term solution for changing the fashion industry, but is great for reducing your own waste – plus, it's fun!

* Go in with an open mind. You never know what you might discover among the tatty fleeces and 1980s shoulder pads. Some of the best treasures in my wardrobe were discovered nestling in the most unlikely places. Do try stuff on too. Items that look iffy on the hanger may look awesome on, or vice versa.

Accept that it requires a certain amount of patience. There'll be the odd occasion where you're hardly through the door before you spot all manner of enticing shirts and shoes, but usually it's more slow-burn in approach – with lots of sifting through rails and exasperated sighs at yet another perfectly nice skirt ruined by too many ruffles, before you hit gold.

 Give everything a good sniff before buying. Some smells can be washed out, but occasionally a particularly heady whiff of sweat and perfume (perfectly preserved from the 1970s) will be hard to shift.

 Don't just look at your particular dress size. Larger items can either be worn purposely oversized – think tunics, wonderfully snuggly jumpers and huge shirts with the sleeves rolled up – or altered to fit a little better.

 In fact, look in the men's section too. It may seem like either everything is either too tiny or gigantic – but in between these two extremes, there are some great blazers, shirts and jumpers to be found. Plus, I swear men's shoes are much better made (especially if you have big feet like me, and spend lots of time sighing sadly at the teeny-weeny pretty vintage heels for women that you'd barely get your big toe in).

 Don't buy just for the sake of it. Accept that, at times, you may walk away empty-handed. However, if you can't stomach the thought of leaving behind a particularly delectable/ridiculous/wonderful item, then consider creating a proper dressing-up box treasure trove for yourself, full of the weirdest and most outrageous things you've found. Did someone say sequins?

Give back too. If you have dresses that are slightly too small or tops that never see the light of day, and they're still in good condition, consider donating them somewhere. Charity shops can always do with more good quality stuff.

WHY CARE ABOUT ALL OF THIS AS A TEENAGER?

I know that I'm lucky to be able to save up and make choices about where I shop. Not everyone has the option to do that. If you're carefully counting your lunch money, then something like this will, of course, not be a priority.

I also think it's harder for teens to buy ethical products. People in their 30s (often the ones sustainable labels are aimed at) have had years of cultivating their wardrobes and can thrive on buying just a few new items each year – or, for some, the kind of job that allows them to afford pricier stuff more often. But as a young person, you're just starting out, just beginning to get your look together. You need things like a wide range of shops to experiment in, the stomach-tingles of a particularly good new outfit – maybe one or two disasters too; impulse buys, things you think will look great but don't; looks to keep up with, items lusted after … When you're busy figuring out all of that, and fashioning yourself in the way you want to be seen, of course the origin of the clothes might matter less.

In your teens you can independently spend money for the first time. Age 13, I thought the height of sophistication was a pair of pink leopard print lace-ups I'd bought in one of the biggest high street chains (a marker, if one was needed, of just how much my outfits have evolved since). Having access to such an amazingly vast array of options was, more than anything else, exciting. The kind of genuine feel-good hit I now get from finding a particularly delectable miniskirt in a charity shop is the same one I used to feel when walking out of a store with one or two choice new items in my branded plastic bag.

I have a whole load of sympathy with those who don't really want to think about where their clothes came from. As Jemima, 17, said to me, *'I'm a teenager, I don't have much income, and it's convenient and cheap – I do feel bad, but at the same time I'm just one person.'*

Meia, 17, had a similar perspective: *'I know they might have been made by girls younger than me who can't go to school because they have to work for a fraction of the money I make, and sometimes I tell myself to never buy them again, but ... you know ... they're cheap!'*

So how to reconcile the awareness with the reality of being a teen? Well, the smallest, most manageable thing I'd encourage is the slightest lifestyle change – one where items of clothing become something you expect to wear plenty of times; chosen because you really like them, rather than being liable to disappear every six months or so to make space for something new.

I cleared out *all* my clothes from my very early teens relatively quickly afterwards – but these days I still wear things I first bought or was given at 14. I've had clear-outs since, but mainly because it no longer fits (anything that sat perfectly on my flat-as-a-sheet-of-paper chest pre-puberty had to go) or because I didn't wear it often enough. But even these haven't been thrown away, they've either been returned to charity shops, or joined my ever-growing pile of things I plan to sell at a vintage fair or online. Minimising wastefulness is a good, practical, thoughtful thing to do, and may mean you enjoy the contents of your wardrobe all the more.

Then, if you're feeling really keen, next time you buy something, scrutinise the label – or send an email to the chain you've just spent your money in, asking where it was made and how their workers are treated. You could even do a little digging around online. Labour Behind the Label is a good website to start with – and War on Want's campaign 'Love Fashion. Hate Sweatshops' is great too.

I ask this, because transparency is still a huuuuge problem when it comes to finding out about clothes. As I mentioned above, it's difficult to discover anything about things like factory standards or worker treatment. The most one might get is a country – 'Bangladesh', quite possibly, or 'Indonesia' or 'Thailand' or any of the other countries Western mega-brands rely on to give them fast shipments and low-cost labour.

Dina, 19, almost echoing my own thoughts, said *'It frustrates me how little we know when we walk into a high street shop,'* but followed it up by noting that *'There is yet to be a fashion brand that is Fairtrade that suits my style.'*

This is another big problem. Although 'ethical fashion' exists and is improving all the time, it isn't perfect – particularly for teens. We're the ones who will be buying clothes for another 70 years or so. You'd think there'd be sustainable labels clamouring for our attention.

But, for us to be interested in spending a little more money than average, it requires a much larger range of clothes to choose from – with more created to appeal to a young market. Pretty, gorgeous, heart-fluttering things that you want to buy because they're so desirable. It seems to me that there are only a handful of great brands at the moment, and very few are producing designs as enticing as those found elsewhere on the high street.

So, for more sustainable designers to do well, we need two things to happen. First, we all need to start to think through how our money is spent, what we value, and who our purchases benefit. We (and I include myself here) still want to spend the minimum amount for the maximum gain. That needs to alter: we need to realign our expectations. Second, as a society, we need to encourage and support high street brands who are trying to do good things, and look towards more independent brands too.

STYLE IS SOMETHING I CARE ABOUT. SO WHAT?

I'm always pulled up short if someone is dismissive of me thanks to the care I've put into my outfit. Look at any online article with a comment chain, and you'll see that the word 'fashion' provokes the grumpiest opinions, as though any interest in what you wear is a flimsy pastime with no real purpose.

Why is this? I often get the sense it is being dismissed as a banal *female* hobby (even though many men love clothes too). It feels as though the commenter is sniffing at those who enjoy the simple pleasure that new clothes or a new look can bring, as if being critical about something as simple as clothing gives them some sort of higher, worthier status.

I've no idea where this idea that style or fashion is dull or frivolous stems from. As far as I'm concerned style is an empowering way to make yourself look different/pretty/powerful/eye-catching/unusual because *you* want to.

There *are* uncomfortable things done in the name of fashion – the insistence that ultimate beauty belongs to young, skinny models; clothes produced by exploiting people and planet; the message that happiness can be found in a new handbag – but these are separate to an interest in personal style. Just because there is a dark side to the fashion industry doesn't mean that the whole subject of fashion and style is tainted or less meaningful as a result. Although there are big issues on all sides of the debate, it doesn't make the clothes themselves – or the pleasure in wearing them – frivolous.

Besides, you can criticise the nasty side of the fashion industry and indulge in buying new, exciting things (hopefully from a non-nasty source). You're allowed to ask questions about beauty standards *and* be thrilled by make-up. In fact, loving the perfect shade of foundation means you're perfectly placed to criticise the industry that produces it – often we engage most strongly with the things we already care about. If you're a passionate believer in the power of cosmetics, why not question digital retouching? If you adore clothes, you are just the person to ask why some designers don't acknowledge that women might actually possess boobs or hips.

> It's taken me a while to realise that I can enjoy putting on eye-shadow and reading the September issue of Vogue, and then have a feminist discussion of advertising with a friend.
>
> Elizabeth, 16

Plus, it's perfectly acceptable to be intelligent or thoughtful or politically aware and still love the feeling of wearing a truly stunning dress. More than acceptable. Kind of awesome. Not caring at all about what you wear? Also awesome. But no matter your age or interests, if you love choosing your outfits, then own it – and if anyone has the audacity to suggest that this makes you vapid or a bimbo, tell them where to shove it (while looking fabulous, of course).

3

THE BIGGEST PLAYGROUND ON EARTH

Remember those girls who were so concerned about my cup size in the lunch queue? I can still recall how nervous I used to get watching them gather round a laptop – I had no idea what they might get up to next. I used to find it frightening that the people I could always rely on for a quick put-down also had the power to Google anything, go anywhere, say whatever they wanted, talk to – or about – whoever they stumbled across. Unlike my own online life, which was pretty self-controlled, the social group mentality of 'how can we piss around?' meant the infinite, never-ending possibilities of the web were both gripping and nerve-racking.

It's funny, considering how much of each day I now spend in front of a screen. Back then, online life seemed both smaller and larger. It had a restricted number of uses: blogging, homework, gaming, a smattering of time on social networks, idle surfing. But it also seemed to stretch in every direction. If you wanted, you could find or access *anything*.

My brother is five years younger than me. The role the internet plays in his life is almost incomparable to what I saw and experienced online at his age. Things evolve quicker than you can catch your breath. A few years ago we shared stuff on our phones via a miraculously free but strange new way of transferring data called Bluetooth, while ideas like Twitter,

Instagram and WhatsApp were still in their infancy.

The problem with even mentioning these last few sites by name is that they may have fallen out of use by the time this is being read. In the same way that it's easy to spot hopelessly outdated attempts to get down wiv da kidz via text speak and slang – something that stopped being cool in the late 2000s, and was *never* cool when said by an adult – making mention of various sites will date what I'm saying immediately. Who knows what will be popular within a year or two?

Yet, although technology and internet trends may be moving faster than a herd of bespectacled hipsters towards the next iPhone, there are still plenty of questions to ask and problems to address. In fact, the breakneck pace of change is at the heart of that. The way we communicate and share information has altered, and continues to alter, year by year – or month by month. It feels like we've barely had time to catch up on things we now consider normal. The net is so central to our lives that it's easy to forget how new all of this is.

Hang on though. If we're talking teens and the internet, surely the discussion is meant to go like this? *Bad bad stranger danger oh it's awful the youth of today bad cyber-bullying bad sexting dreadful bad privacy controls oh bad they're all brain-dead from too much time online bad it was better in my day ban it ALL.*

This overreaction does little to help. A few of the ideas woven up in these breathless cries are important. Stuff like bullying and maintaining your privacy and staying safe are serious and are, all too frequently, the reason people get hurt (there's a reason for lots of the rule making). But to suggest that the sum total of teens' online life is a great long list of awful scariness? Ridiculous.

Beyond the doom and gloom, there are all sorts of amazing and creative ways to engage with the internet: through coding, building websites, developing apps, making videos and vlogging, writing blogs, socialising, finding new friends and playing games.

Sometimes the world online can be a lifeline too – a way of realising that you're not alone, and there are almost definitely others out there experiencing the same things you are going through. Take Rowan, 19, who talked about the fantastic support networks online for transgender teens. She said to me, '*I started to reach out to queer communities online in my mid-teens ... without that resource I would never have been able to come out as a trans woman.*'

There's a ton of creative resources too. Think of *Rookie* – the online mag founded by Tavi Gevinson, with loads of fabulous contributors and a constantly updated contents list stretching from first kisses to DIY false eyelashes. I wish it had been around when I was younger. It's smart, funny, thoughtful and creative. We need more media like that, both online and in print, and it's getting easier to find now.

The internet is so full of potential. All those opportunities for connecting, creating, finding like-minded people, staying in touch with old friends, making new ones, learning, networking are awesome. Overwhelmingly awesome.

MAKING FRIENDS ONLINE

Last summer I stayed with a friend who lives in another country and I'd met once, briefly, simply because we liked each other's tweets.

Meia, 17

Some of my favourite people are ones I first met online. I have friends of all ages who I wouldn't know without my blog or other social media platforms. The internet has given me work opportunities, wonderful conversations and a space where I could be taken seriously.

The internet can be a place ripe for forming friendships. Yas, 17, said to me, '*I know they tell you not to meet people online, but pretty much all of my good friendships were found there!*' Meeting people online is more and more the norm, meaning we need to re-evaluate how we define stranger danger. It's no longer enough to say 'never meet up with anyone you get chatting to online'. It has to be more nuanced. Any conversation must acknowledge that there are communities and people to chat to – and that some of them may become close friends (how wonderful is that?) – but that there are also some nasties out there. So how to go about tackling all this sensibly?

✱ First, when you're online, check the info your new friend provides about themselves – do you have friends in common? Are there pictures? Do these pictures tell a complete story? Are they present on other forms of social media?

✻ Listen to your gut if anything seems even remotely dodgy or off-key, and be careful about what you reveal about yourself and whether it makes you easily traceable.

✻ Let your parents know about anyone new that you're talking to. If you really can't bear the thought of keeping them updated on your social habits then find someone else responsible. Friends don't necessarily have the same insight – or the same uh-oh-ometer. Also, even if everything does seem right and dandy, don't stop being cautious.

✻ If you want to move the conversation offline and meet up, do so in a very public, busy place. Take an older mate or family member along. In the future, make sure other people know where you are and when you'll be back.

✻ Basically, listen to your instincts, try not to leave yourself vulnerable, remove yourself from any situation where you're feeling uncomfortable, never ever agree to meet at that person's house or anywhere else behind a closed door, and keep someone else in the loop.

✻ As long as you take a responsible attitude – and why wouldn't you – there's no reason why the internet shouldn't be your new friend-finder.

PUT YOUR BEST FACE FORWARD

There is something extra fun about meeting up with someone you met online for the first time: How are they going to match up with the person you've been piecing together from their no-doubt carefully curated selfies and declared love of 1990s teen flicks and 8-bit video games?

What we wear and how we behave changes between different social groups or situations, whether it's speaking at an event, messing around with mates, going on a date or negotiating a tricky family meal. We're always presenting versions of ourselves – deciding what to show, what to hide, when to crack filthy jokes, when to be polite. They're all the same person, but from slightly altered angles. Now nearly all of us have some kind of online identity too (or several). But are they as easy to turn on and off?

Your online identity is presented through the words and images you've chosen to share – whether that means splurging everything on your homepage or carefully considering each statement and snap. But can we divide online from offline, or virtual from in the flesh? 'IRL' may be an annoying acronym, but it shows how we still like to distinguish between internet life and 'real' life.

Ok, I think most of us have figured out the internet is real too, but we do tend to have a heightened self-consciousness online – an awareness of how we're viewing and being viewed by others through our screens. This can give us the chance to create a very strong identity and set of interests. We can always say the perfect line or deliver the ideally timed dramatic insight online that, let's face it, we'd never be able to deliver off the cuff. Yet there are also downsides. Everyone else is only presenting their best side too, and that is easy to forget.

Something like the selfie represents the problems that come with this whole viewing-and-being-viewed thing. On the one hand there's the wonder of being able to cultivate a reflection of yourself, taking control of how you're represented – perhaps proving that it's ok to be proud of feeling that you look good. I enjoy the creative aspect to a good selfie as much as the next person. On the other side there's the pressure to trim this reflection to meet certain standards – a kind of competition to look a certain way, fit the pre-made moulds, get the most flattery.

A lot of us feel like Amy, 14, who said to me, *'I think on my Instagram there is this prettier person with photos of sections of my life, which I'd like to preserve as my image of who I am.'* She went on to explain how she'd measure herself against this 'perfect self' she'd put online, feeling that the real, everyday her didn't always match up. How many of us have felt exactly the same way? Like if we just added a crop here and a filter there, our looks – or life – could be improved a little? There are even apps that will do a rickety version of retouching any flaws unworthy of a selfie, quietly supporting the possibility that you can – and maybe even should – construct a better, more attractive you online.

THE SELFIE SELF

What those retouching/flaw-hiding apps underline to me is a typical double standard that the topic of body image is rife with: as much as you're meant to be gorgeous, you're also supposed to be slightly dissatisfied. There's a strong cultural message that we should be hot – but also feel like we're lacking something, or at least play down any pride in our appearance. This weird double-expectation is powerful: look gorgeous, but don't be proud of it. Pout at the camera, but don't be too comfortable in your skin. Be confident, but not enough to scare off the boys. Be sexy, but only for others' eyes – not for your own satisfaction ('cos then you're a slut). Ugh.

It's not surprising then that some young women post captions like 'SO UGLY' under their selfies. A lot of people dismiss this as a plea for attention, because saying something like 'I hate my face' asks for others to contradict that. But why are those kinds of comments made at all? Maybe because the person posting the pic just needs a bit of reassurance. Dismissing this behaviour as attention grabbing puts all the fault on the person who has posted the image and ignores the strange net they are caught in. I think everyone's self-esteem has taken a hit from time to time, and this feeling can only be worsened by the relentless message that you are the sum of your looks, rather than your personality or achievements.

Although 'she's just doing it for attention' may be the ultimate put-down, on some level most of us like a bit of attention from time to time. I still occasionally update my Facebook profile photo when my confidence levels are lower than usual. Why? Because I know it'll provide a lovely little ego-boost. It's pretty standard human behaviour to like being acknowledged by others, to appreciate when they say nice things. However, there's a fine line between enjoying reassurance and craving it which is all-too-easily crossed, particularly if you've been left vulnerable by what's happening in other areas of your life.

The desire to become one with your perfect selfie self can be taken to an extreme. Jenny, 16, spoke to me about how after being bullied, she'd hide behind an impression of flawlessness: *'I'd spend hours and hours of my day researching what teenagers did.'* She'd spend hours researching online make-up tutorials and doing her hair. *'I became like this super-teenage-plastic-mutant,'* she says. Maintaining this image was exhausting. *'More often than not I was being complimented on social media on how perfect I was,'* she continues, *'getting 200+ likes on each photo. It was a huge reputation to keep up when I felt as though I was crumbling.'*

Most of us don't crumble. Jenny's story *is* an extreme response. But the maintenance of a particular appearance, an identity, a reputation, can take its toll. Selfies and imagery, so full of potential to enhance confidence, don't always allow us to celebrate ourselves in the best possible way. They can make us forget the zillions of other amazing things we do and are capable of doing outside the framed edges. Instead the message becomes that we *are* our bodies and faces – and these should be held up for approval.

SOME GREAT FEMALE SELFIE ARTISTS ⋙➤

Is there a difference between a selfie and a self-portrait? I began thinking about self-portraits when I first studied Frida Kahlo for my art GCSE. Her arresting paintings, exploring disturbing and difficult aspects of her own life, hit me in a very personal way. She'd hurt her spine badly following a traffic accident as a young woman. In one image, she replaced her vertebrae with a crumbling stone column. She had tears running down her cheeks. It made me cry too, so evocative was it of my own twisted spine, which had been straightened into a column of its own six months before. Kahlo once said, *'I am the subject I know best'* – taking control of her own image in painting after painting.

✱ Sanaa Hamid

(British Asian, born 1992) Rising star Sanaa Hamid often uses herself as the starting point for questioning cultural, religious and ethnic identities and expectations in thought provoking and even funny ways.

✱ Francesca Woodman

(American, born 1958) Even when taking photos of herself age 13, Woodman used the camera to explore her identity, gender and body. During her tragically short lifetime, she often posed in abandoned spaces, with slow shutter speeds blurring the images.

✱ Cindy Sherman

(American, born 1954) One of the most important contemporary artists, whether she's mimicking fashion imagery or film stills, her self-portraits are both unsettling and provocative.

🗷 Amrita Sher-Gil

(Indian, born 1913) Growing up in India and moving to Paris aged 16, she embraced Parisian bohemianism, and mixed European and Indian influences in her artwork. Her self-portraits often questioned the way the female body was viewed.

🗷 Artemisia Gentileschi

(Italian, born 1593) An incredible painter, who like many current female artists, received less recognition than her male counterparts, and saw emphasis put on her gender and life story rather than her artwork.

DO YOU DOCUMENT EVERY DETAIL?

Aside from pictures of yourself, the internet encourages a need to capture everything else too. Friends, pets, holidays. I was going to introduce this section by making a joke along the lines of 'if a tree falls in the middle of a wood, and no one Instagrams it, did it really happen?' – but I've already seen several other people tweet similar variations. It's hard to be original when you're surrounded by so many people trying to be funny (and mostly being much funnier than you).

I often catch myself trying to capture and publicise things – novels I've read, trips I've had, outfits I've worn. Why? Partly because everyone else does. But there's also this compulsion to let others know what you're up to – as though you'll disappear if you don't constantly have other people confirm that, yes, you exist and you've got some great eyeliner on today.

It's usually the good bits that end up online. The flattering pictures, the pretty cupcakes, the takeaway coffee cup, the nails just painted – not all the in-between stuff where you're feeling crap about the way someone is treating you, or the fact that your room is looking like a pigsty – albeit a rather elegant pigsty full of shoes and clothes rather than mud.

It's fine to carefully choose which parts of yourself you open up online. In fact, it's healthy. It gives a divide between the private and the public, allowing each of us to control what others see. Take a look at my Instagram and there'll be bookshelves, clothes, art and curios aplenty. Occasionally a snap of a friend. Perhaps more selfies than strictly necessary. But properly personal stuff? Not very often.

As I've just shown, most of us know exactly what we're selecting, and concealing. But not all of us extend that awareness to other people. We recognise that our own interior life stretches far beyond anything posted online. Yet with others we respond purely to what is seen, assuming that it stands in for the whole. It's rare to consider how everyone else is thinking just as carefully about their artful shots of chai lattes, their poses with mates, their constant suggestions that all their nights out are *just the best*.

This has done something interesting to celebrity culture too. If we're busy presenting ourselves to each other, famous people are presenting themselves to the wider world. In one sense, it brings us nearer to famous individuals. We can read their thoughts, see them in their candid moments. Really? Hmm ... well, no, not really. Yes, there are celebs who manage their own social media and are very genuine in what they put out. But there are plenty who have very carefully cultivated personas. Every seemingly casual selfie will be meticulously put together, each tweet considered by a PR team before it's published. There are plenty of hidden strings behind the polished front (and some weighty money bags too).

And even if their shares are genuine, it doesn't mean that you have any more access to the person. Because you can see a celebrity publishing their thoughts in real time or posting snaps from their holidays, it seems like you know them, but it's nearly all entirely one-way. This illusion of access is a strange state of affairs where we're both closer to and further away from those we admire.

BEWARE THE OVERSHARE

There is another side to this careful cultivation – overshare. We've all had that one friend – or had moments of being that friend – who posts about 300 new clubbing pics a week, or constantly broadcasts what a pain in the arse their mum is, or a million pictures of their recent shopping spree. Whether it is too-often shared updates, too many pictures, or just too much information about exploits the night before, there's no discrimination, just a kind of splurge with little or no thought of the consequences.

With overshare of images – particularly where they include other people, it's always worth asking others before uploading.

As tempting as it is to put online every single image of your friends you've ever taken, including all the ones where they're pulling stupid faces or snogging someone in the corner, will they want others to see them? It's good manners to find out – and also, crucially, to check what their take is on being tagged in photos too.

There's an extra issue with this spilling of everything in a big, messy, unedited state too – depending on privacy settings (or sometimes not), anyone, anywhere could see it all. Just because no one is commenting or responding, doesn't mean they're not looking. How many times have you Facebook-stalked someone or found their blog? (Just me?)

Also, even if people are not looking right now, it doesn't mean they won't in future. I have friends who regret the amount of personal information they posted online when they were younger. All it takes is a quick Google to locate their previous vulnerabilities, their 15-year-old thoughts, their blurry, drunken pictures. Images can be deleted, but traces will remain. Bea, 14, says *'When I put a photo up online, it's always something I'd be comfortable with in the future – you know, if it turned up in a collection of photos at my wedding.'*

It's also helpful to remember that anything has the potential to be reblogged, retweeted or shared pretty much infinitely. Obviously, this doesn't happen to the vast majority of content on the web, but that possibility is always there. Being truly conscious of the longevity of anything on the internet is an easy lesson hard won: you should always be aware of what you're uploading and who could access it.

The bog-standard advice is to not put up anything you wouldn't be happy for your grandma to see. Frankly, that's patronising and out of touch. Plus, it suggests that all grandparents are sweet, little, elderly, white-haired people who might be shocked at the sight of some bare flesh or (oh goodness me, fetch the smelling salts!) swear words. Funnily enough, even octogenarians were young once too, and probably got up to *all* sorts of things that'd make your toes curl if they started telling you in any great detail. My grandma is a cool lady.

Maybe we need to reframe sharing, make it more about retaining your own power rather than worrying about it being in the hands of someone else (granny or otherwise). In fact, safety in general should be aimed at enjoying the great stuff without leaving yourself vulnerable. Olivia, 15, says *'my Mum was telling me that when she was my age, she'd write in diaries how she felt. She bought me my own a while ago. I used to put things up on Facebook. I forgot that people could see what I was uploading. Then I realised that it's not a good idea. Now I put my personal stuff in the diary. Then nobody can see it unless I want them to.'*

While writing this book, I did a bit of research into what organisations and the government say about overshare and privacy. Scrolling through websites and videos devoted to safety, I was struck by how many of them had barely moved on from the kinds of lectures I got at age 14, despite how vastly evolved technology has become since then. Who thought that continuing to use '2 u' instead of 'to you' would miraculously make teenagers go, 'Ah, yes, I should not sext or give information to strangers. These safety people get me. They understand my lingo. I will listen to them'?

This disconnect between the ones providing the information and those who need it is strange. There's little designed to engage with teens. A better example is Oii my Size, an initiative developed by young women (supported by the organisation Peabody) to tackle communication between girls and boys. Their website is engaging because it takes young people and their problems seriously. More of that please.

DID YOU DOWNLOAD THIS BOOK FOR FREE?

To move swiftly on to another type of sharing, a quick question. Was this book downloaded for free? If you're reading print, this is easy and the answer is short: no (unless you found, downloaded, and then printed out and bound the entire thing yourself – which seems like an enormous amount of effort).

If you've got a screen in front of your nose, then thank you ever so much if you actually bought this. If you found my book online for free, then ... well ... I'm a little sad. It's a generational thing, sure. With it being easy to download music for free (often illegally, when music first went online), of course it was going to happen to other forms of media too. But behind every finished song or published book there's a team who've worked on it – not just the creator, but all the others who've contributed.

All of them need to make a living. We don't expect plumbers to give their services for free, or teachers to come into the classroom purely out of the goodness of their own hearts. Just because people who write/take photos/make music/work on films aren't necessarily in an office, doesn't mean their skills aren't worth paying for.

A while ago, an image of me ended up in a luxury property company brochure – they'd lifted it from a website where I'd been featured during London Fashion Week. The quote they superimposed over me – 'style is always in fashion' – was horrendously clichéd, and the principle infuriating. There are so many companies who treat the internet like a free-for-all, running wild like rich kids in a sweet shop.

I'm pretty sure that the majority of people reading this aren't into developing luxury properties, but most people are used to sharing others' images online. And so do you give credit where credit is due? As a blogger, I can't express how important it is to credit other people's work if you are using it on your blog: give the source a name and link to their site (and, ideally, get permission too). Similar to the 'just bloody pay' principle for stuff that has a price tag, treating content that is free with due respect is just a generally decent way to conduct yourself online.

✳ Rosianna Halse Rojas: ✸ The Vlogger

With her videos covering everything from feminist gift guides to the importance of being good to yourself, it's worth checking out **@papertimelady**. When she's not making videos, she works as YA author John Green's PA.

How did you find your teenage years?

I felt like my teenage years were one big test and the only possible results were pass or fail. That impression came from school and from home but it also came from myself: I had a huge part to play in creating the impossible expectations I placed upon myself, and looking back I often think I set things up so that I would feel like a failure. I struggled with depression and body image issues but refused help when it was offered. I'm still horribly stubborn, but I try to focus more on self-care.

When did you stop feeling like a teenager?

Does 19 count as teenage? If it does, the last of my teenage years left me feeling incredibly isolated after my dad died suddenly of a stroke while I was thousands of miles away on holiday. That was my 'right, I have to be a proper adult now' moment.

Why did you choose YouTube?

YouTube becomes a good forum for talking about feminism and identity because the commentary does not privilege the videomaker's point of view. Generally speaking, most vloggers edit their own videos and do not have to deal with middlemen before putting it up, which means it's less likely that what they want to say will be distorted by someone else ... That's huge.

How do you balance the work you do (vlogs, being John Green's PA, contributing to things like Sheryl Sandberg's Lean In: For Graduates)?

Doing many different jobs doesn't leave a lot of free time but I've never really known what to do with free time. I get very restless, very easily and am – perhaps slightly unhealthily? – focused on being as productive with my day as possible. Working across various mediums is wonderful because I don't feel limited to one field, one subject matter, one mode of expression or communication, and I take things I've learnt from my work with John and put them into my videos or my writing and vice versa.

Why did you start the Ladies Survey ?

I started the Ladies Survey after my friend Lex and I produced the first #womenonyoutube panel at VidCon and had an amazing response. We talked about trolls, online hate, harassment, stalking, and some of the other experiences women have online in droves. These things put off women from becoming creators or participating in comments, and dissuade existing creators from continuing. As a result, we risk being in a position where we do not hear women's stories and voices, and in a world where women's voices are already shut out. Lex and I felt strongly that we need to work against the creation of a YouTube culture in which women are neither seen nor heard.

What was the effect?

After we finished the panel, we all had an amazing amount of positive energy to channel into creating supportive networks of women and proposing changes for the website, but I also had an overwhelming sense that we hadn't heard enough. The Ladies Survey allowed the conversation to continue and it does slowly feel like some sort of progress is being made because more people are taking part and more women feel comfortable and safe enough to share their experiences with the internet.

CYBERBULLYING

It's an odd word, really, isn't it? 'Cyberbullying'. There's more than a whiff of 1970s *Doctor Who* there, conjuring up images of whirring cogs or aliens constructed from tinfoil and kitchen implements. I guess it's useful to describe the ways in which technology has enabled a heightened and relentless type of bullying. But calling it 'cyber' separates it off from 'real life' bullying. Bullying is bullying, whether it's on a screen or in person. And often the two combine.

> *My therapist told me to delete Ask.fm, but then I started to go back on it. There were really bad ones in Year Seven – when I didn't realise I had depression – telling me to drink bleach, to kill myself. It made me less confident. I went to school, thinking one of the people in this room might have sent that – didn't know who to trust, who to talk to.*
>
> *Olivia, 15*

One of the more frustrating consequences of this distinction between on- and offline bullying is that the standard response to cyberbullying is to actually punish the victim – to force them to go without access to a particular website or limit their phone time. This places the responsibility on the one hurt, rather than the ones doing the hurting. People are ready to address the effect with no thought of cause.

Big companies like Twitter and Ask.fm are becoming much better at rooting out unsafe behaviour and harmful comments: and hopefully they'll get ever better at listening to victims.

Cyberbullying is horribly pervasive. When so much of our lives are played out online, having that space compromised by people who wish you ill is horrendous. Phones and screens mean we're connected nearly ALL the time, leaving greater room for others to be vile. It makes me sad that with every updated, marvellous form of technology, people prove their ability to be little shits in new and innovative ways. But what's put up online can have consequences – serious ones.

Kelly, 15, goes to a single-sex school, and described to me how the teachers took a novel approach to online hate. *'People would slag off each other on the internet all the time. They'd put whatever came into their head online,'* she says. She told me how all the year groups were called into an assembly out of the blue, teachers standing silent at the sides of the hall. After playing a YouTube clip about Amanda Todd – the young woman who took her own life, aged 15, in 2012 following a vicious cyberbullying campaign – they began flashing up other things on-screen.

'First of all I didn't realise it was from girls in our school,' Kelly continues. *'I thought it was just horrible stuff, judgements, gossip. But it started mentioning teachers' names – then students. It was a PowerPoint naming and shaming everyone who had bitched about other people. It was awful. We were all*

watching as these messages came up. Everyone was shocked and embarrassed.' Making it personal meant it delivered a powerful kick. *'Parents got really angry afterwards, and students said, "I can't believe they were stalking" but this was all online, anyone could find it.'* I asked her whether it actually had an impact, and she thought it had: *'Most people realised that what they were doing was nasty – previously they'd thought it was harmless.'*

If cyberbullying happens to you, what can you do? Well, screen-cap and record things and keep a log – and don't delete messages or images you've been sent. Mainly though, the advice is the same for any kind of bullying: tell someone – no matter how afraid or scared you might feel about doing so. It can be hard to let people know that you're being bullied, but trying to tackle it yourself can leave you feeling more isolated than ever.

Whether you approach a teacher yourself or let your parents do that is up to you, but please talk to someone who is equipped to help you. If it's serious, repeated abuse, they can report it to the police, who can contact website or network providers – and possibly identify the ones behind it. Depending on how awful the bullying is, it may come under the 1997 Harassment Act.

Some of the best charities to help out are the well-known (but still ever so wonderful) ones like the NSPCC and ChildLine. Another useful organisation to know about is the CEOP – the Child Exploitation and Online Protection Centre. As well as the task of dealing with some really dreadful stuff, they're behind the website ThinkUKnow.co.uk which delivers sound advice.

I'd also suggest Cybersmile as a very good, very helpful website. They were set up to explicitly tackle cyberbullying, and you can tell. The website is slick, their social media presence is great, and they give all sorts of avenues for support and help. More places now are working with mentor schemes – where those who have been cyberbullied themselves can then help or talk to others in a similar position.

COULD YOU BE AN ONLINE BULLY?

Bullying is often described as something totally conscious, as though 'The Bully' (that stock character of so many books and films and cartoons) wakes up each morning, thinking, 'Aaah, how shall I bully today? What methods of torture now? It's bullying time!' Although that may happen now and again, it's far more common that the person in the wrong simply doesn't realise how damaging their words or actions are.

Here are some common justifications for bullying behaviour that I've stumbled across. Have you ever heard yourself think or say one of these phrases?

It was just a joke!
Ever heard the expression, 'Comedy is tragedy happening to someone else'? We may not be talking Greek drama here, but what may seem absolutely hilarious to everyone else won't

always be that funny for whoever's on the receiving end. If entertainment comes at the price of someone feeling bloody miserable, is it really that much fun?

I didn't mean it!

Sometimes we put things up online without fully thinking through the consequences. That tagged image or message tapped out in a flash may not have had much consideration. But on the internet, things are pretty permanent – meaning a throwaway comment could do some considerable damage.

She should get over it/He should get a thicker skin

It's easy to imagine how we would react if faced with our own jokes or snarky comments, but would you truly think it was nothing if someone, perhaps anonymously, was attempting to make your life feel a little (or a lot) more horrible?

Well, it's only online – not like it's real life or anything

Although being distanced by a screen may make it feel like other people don't properly exist, or don't have feelings, they do. The way the laptop illuminates the dark room? How a phone fits snugly into the palm of a hand? It's the same for everyone else. We're all connected. We're all real people. Words will have an effect, regardless of whether it's face-to-face or online.

It doesn't matter to her – she's got better marks/friends/clothes/parents than me

Aah, a little honesty emerges. Now we're getting somewhere. Envying someone is easy – but responding nastily rather than working out what's behind your dissatisfaction won't help: what's *really* bugging you? And what can you do in your own life to fix that lack? Also: who knows what private struggles others are already going through? Most of the time, we have little idea of what those around us are facing. Maybe their life isn't quite as enviable as you think.

NO LOLS TROLLS

It had already been happening for years, but trolling really hit the headlines when lots of women in the public eye began speaking up about the kinds of appalling messages they were receiving (and who knows how many people faced these kind of attacks without any media coverage).

I'm not going to reduce trolls down to spotty school kids picking their noses or middle-aged IT workers with stale lives – not because there aren't trolls like that, but because it turns them into typecasts (the process is begun by calling them trolls rather than morons or idiots or insert swear words here). In the same way that horror movies build the baddies into big, terrifying beasts, so we want our internet trolls to look like sadsack, pimply, slightly pale, dandruff-ridden creatures more like Gollum than functional members of the human race.

But anyone can troll. Mothers, brothers, stressed workers, bullied girls, messed-up teenagers. Some are sick, having genuine psychological problems, or may have something deeply difficult causing problems in their own life. All sorts of things can cause nasty behaviour; it can be found everywhere, and it tends to fester in the cracks of the internet like a bad case of dry rot. It's classic bullying – a power rush of manipulation and meanness, one man making himself feel better by making others feel worse.

Here's how trolling makes someone feel: nervous. The day that was going well, airy and clear, suddenly has a black spot on the corner of it. Not a big one. Just a speck. But it's a weighty speck, letting that person know that someone out there is intending them some kind of malice. If there are lots of people trolling? The specks get bigger and bigger until they're taking up all attention, massing into a blot that spreads and clouds vision.

Often it's brushed off by others from the outside as 'nothing personal'... just for the lulz. And to an extent it's not personal, in that it has no bearing on you as a person or in how you live your life. But I don't think that's quite what the naysayers are getting at. Instead it's the age-old message 'get over yourself'. Because apparently to feel, to admit that something has thrown you, that your body had a physical reaction – is to admit to being weak.

Some are now so used to trolling and threats that they bounce off with all the ineffectuality of rubber bullets aimed at full body armour. But regardless of whether it's brushed off or deeply felt it's another one of those scenarios where the victim is blamed. 'Just ignore them'/ 'don't respond '/ 'rise above it'/ 'you do seem to bringing it on yourself now by talking about it'. It does work for some – ignoring behaviour can be a good way of showing you're not affected. Deciding not to engage at all is a totally valid thing to do. But that doesn't mean anyone can or should tell the victims who've decided to voice their anger at being targeted that they're making it worse for themselves. Those voices are important. They need to be heard, supported and amplified. Not shut down with some snide 'don't feed the trolls' one-liner.

We need more empathy on the internet. In fact, to go full-on rainbows and unicorns, we just need more empathy as humans, full-stop – more awareness of how others feel, how what we say could hurt them, and perhaps a responsibility towards looking after, supporting and standing up for those who've been attacked. A type of empathy that involves an awful lot of listening to others, and looking to experiences beyond our own, rather than seeing who can shout the loudest.

Sanne Vliegenthart: The Book Vlogger

Sanne Vliegenthart is a book vlogger (username: 'booksandquills'). She works in publishing as a social media manager, and is a general advocate of all things excitingly bookish.

Do you remember the key moment where you thought, 'I'm going to begin vlogging'?

It started building when I discovered the Vlogbrothers, John and Hank Green, at the end of 2007. Right after that, the Five Awesome Girls channel started – these were five girls around my age, that liked all of the same things I liked, and I thought 'Well, if they can do it …' Those people were cool, and it seemed that the only way I could be a part of that was to start making videos myself and join this community of creators.

So you now work in social media – first for Hot Key Books and now for Penguin Random House. Could you outline what the nature of your job is?

I manage social media platforms for publishers. At Hot Key, I was doing all the video creation (I made more than a hundred!)

and a lot of my job was getting authors and team members to be comfortable on camera. I was doing all the social media channels there, but I'm focusing on YouTube and Facebook at Penguin. Whatever shape it takes, it's about finding readers, reaching out, and getting them excited about new books.

It's wonderful that you seem to have translated something you LOVE into something that pays the bills. Any thoughts on that?

What I really like about this job is that I'm coming from a point where I've already tried stuff out on my own channel, or I've seen other people do it. I've received some training from Google over the years, but mostly I'm completely self-taught. It's interesting to bring that from a personal perspective to a company perspective.

That's so true. It seems easy to underestimate just how far you can get by doing creative, savvy things online, and where that can take you careers-wise ...

I've been doing it for over seven years now. Without realising, you're learning and improving all the time. You don't go into creating a YouTube channel thinking, 'I'm going to acquire so many useful skills.' You go, 'Ok, I want to create a video – what do I do?' Get your hands on a camera, figure out what editing software is, how it works, where to download it. Later, you realise you're good at public speaking, photography, editing, storytelling … All gained while having fun.

You recommended Chimamanda Ngozi Adichie's _We Should All Be Feminists_ in a video – are there any other books you think people should read if they're interested in feminism?

I'm currently reading _Everyday Sexism_. It's a really good one to open your eyes to things that people usually just sweep under the rug. Obviously, I like _Lean In_ by Sheryl Sandberg. I've got a few on my to-read list too. I've heard great things about _Bad Feminist_ by Roxane Gay. I don't think all feminist reading needs to be non-fiction though. Just reading widely and diversely and seeking different accounts of experiences can be possibly even more useful than specific books on feminism.

USING THE INTERNET RATHER THAN LETTING IT USE YOU

One of the things I will be eternally grateful for is how useful a tool Twitter was while writing this book. It not only led me to all sorts of fantastic articles to read and organisations to contact, but also brought me plenty of teens to talk to. It's amazing how far a request for interviewees can travel.

The second reason I was grateful for this was my sudden realisation that, thank god, all my time online hadn't been wasted! The hours spent scrolling, procrastinating and idly lingering hadn't all been in vain ...

I've been in a constant battle with my internet consumption since I was 15. Having a blog has been a blessing, but between that and doing a degree in English, and a lot of writing, my activities require huge amounts of screen time. Even when you've got a deadline fast roaring towards you, it can be ever so hard to resist the temptation to hover the mouse over the browser rather than the Word document where it should be stationed. With another three pages to go, the desire to suddenly look up obscure singers on YouTube becomes all the more alluring. (In fact, after finishing that sentence I just checked Facebook ... and maybe my blog too ... and perhaps the news as well).

I do worry that there's all this time I could have spent doing other, more useful things than seeing how much old classmates have changed or looking at someone else's online spat. To be fair to myself, a lot of it is constructive though – reading, thinking, emailing, responding, discussing, celebrating others.

It doesn't help though that our brains are wired in such a way that the internet can quickly become addictive. Seeing notifications or icons letting you know that somewhere in the world someone has contacted you, even if it is only a spammer offering Viagra at bargain prices, delivers a shot of the addictive happiness hormone, dopamine, to the brain's pleasure-centre. I think of it as being similar to what you get with a sugar-rush – that satisfaction of the sweet hit and increased energy, followed by the slump when you've consumed too much.

You have to decide what kind of role technology plays in your day-to-day life. For a few, it's already minimal. For a lot of people it requires plenty of willpower not to be constantly seeking updates. But even if it's as small a step as not checking every single social media platform before you've got out of bed, it's something.

> *I love that my blog gives me the ability to share my voice and express myself creatively. But it's really important to be aware of how easy it is to get caught up in social media. I need to remind myself that the internet cannot replace real-life experiences.*
>
> *Willow, 16* (◁

Essentially, the internet is a marvellous resource, and a grotesque one, responsible for great good – and plenty of evil.

Friendships and bullying. Innovation and distraction. Amazing information and overwhelmingly disturbing content. Fresh relationships and borderline harassment. New, much-needed voices and trolling. Entertainment and trash. Enhanced opportunities and malicious hacking. Even referring to it as 'the internet' feels odd – somehow archaic, as though it's separate from the rest of life. It's ingrained now. No going back. But much of the way we consume and use it is done without question, without examining just what we're doing – and what the consequences are.

The trick is also to harvest all the best bits. We have so many opportunities that have never been available before. More chance to waste time, yes, but more chance for the most marvellous possibilities too. As much as I may occasionally envy my mum's tech-free teenage years, complete with their spontaneous road trips and long walks and willingness to strike up conversations with strangers, I have to remind myself that without the internet, my own social circle would be hugely diminished. I wouldn't be writing this book. I also wouldn't have a blog, wouldn't be constantly finding work opportunities and new friendships online, wouldn't be able to research anything I wanted within a click or two, wouldn't be able to find trivial info and tremendous opportunities, wouldn't know anywhere near the same amount about inequality or world issues. It'd be a life lacking so much of what I now value. So really, I have to be grateful. And then also spend a little less time on Twitter.

NOTES ON FAMILY

4

HOW I LEARNED TO MISS MY FAMILY

I only began to realise how much I valued my parents when I left for uni. Age 16 or 17, I'd looked forward rather gleefully to the independence and self-sufficiency of being away from home – convinced life would be one long string of new social engagements and magnificent evenings.

These did eventually come about (fitted around the relentless pace of study and work), but I didn't factor in all the mornings where I'd wake up and not quite know what to do with myself, or the evenings where I'd suddenly feel the pang of not getting to sit down for dinner, everyone taking the piss out of each other as we cracked jokes. I wasn't homesick. I was family-sick.

I'm immensely fortunate to have grown up in an environment where stories, conversation, laughter and honesty formed the backbone of our home life. Both my parents are self-employed, so I've been used to the fairly consistent presence of at least one of them at home, something I value all the more in retrospect. There have been incredibly challenging times, yes (more on that later), plenty of shouting, and a continual stream of low-level bickering, but we muddle through.

In general we're a family of long, weekend breakfasts, mid-morning coffee breaks and late-night chats; of Dad leading us on lengthy Sunday walks (usually ensuring we get lost and end up trekking down a stream, or something equally annoying) and Mum taking me on charity shop trips. My younger brother veers between silent and raucous. We're a small unit, lacking much in the way of extended family, but we've formed our own circles of friends and loved ones instead.

Trying to summarise my family is an interesting exercise in stitching together details. What makes us up? Is it our heights – my dad towering above us at six foot eight inches, my mum's five foot six inches looking minuscule by comparison? (I'm an inch off six foot, and I'm positive my brother is going to overtake me soon, which I'm not looking forward to.) Is it our groans at Dad's constant repetition of anecdotes; Mum's never-ending frustration at the way our home is always edged with clutter; my brother's eye-rolls when he's asked how his day at school was?

I think one of the things that helps to bind us together is an almost extraordinary narrative of loss, trauma and love across the past generations. My family's past history has made our current life seem all the more important to protect. Our shared sense that it is a fragile life we lead has made us all the closer in the here and now. We've collectively adopted a dark sense of humour about the less-than-bright side of life.

Neither my mum nor my dad had the easiest of times, especially not as teens. My mum's mum (my late grandma) began adulthood by kicking back against her strict parents. She seemed desperate to escape them after they'd forced her to break off an engagement to a young man they deemed unsuitable because he was from a different religious background. She defiantly rushed into marrying my sweet, late grandfather instead, even though their personalities were incompatible – mostly as a means of spiting her parents. She left him when my mum was still a baby. Later on, she remarried several times, each new husband more of a challenge for my mother than the last. During her teenage years, my mum lived with one particularly nasty stepfather, whose psychologically abusive behaviour transformed her generally happy home life into a constant pattern of walking on eggshells, treading soft steps around a bullying, manipulative man.

My dad's mum is a Czech refugee; the family fled their country in 1948 following the communist coup d'état (they skied over the border disguised as ski tourists). Later she found the first love of her life in my grandfather – who heartbreakingly took his own life when my dad was just a toddler. It was an act that left my grandma without her adored partner, and their two sons fatherless. For my gran the loss was devastating. Both boys were also deeply affected by their father's death, and grew into teenagers stumbling around in a fog of self-medicating addiction. Alcohol and weed for my dad, heroin for his brother. Both got clean and sober when relatively young, but the uncle I would never meet – my dad's only sibling – died in his early 30s. He contracted HIV from a girlfriend, in the dark days when the kinds of medication now available to prevent AIDS weren't around.

These are very brief summaries; they ignore all the nuance and strands of these stories – the glitter that accompanied the hard times. There are so many other tales to tell: my paternal grandma's career as an actress; the days when my grandma lived on a smallholding with my mum, killing their own chickens for dinner, milking the goat, rearing petulant geese, and taking in waifs and strays (animals and people); all these things contribute to the fierce, burning bonds of affection on both sides of my family. But the upshot of these condensed histories is this: when my parents had children, they made a conscious decision to do things their own way, to provide an environment woven out of security and openness and stability.

To return to those first few months at uni then ... the dislocation I felt so strongly at the beginning had its roots in being pulled away from the chatter and sanctuary of home. This is natural. That's how it's meant to be, even if it is difficult to get through. It's part of the process of growing up, becoming more adult, slowly shedding the skin of those younger years.

Although I may see them less, I still talk to my family lots when I'm away, and love their company during the holidays – even as I spend less and less time in our family house. Now I have two homes: one in a tiny village in the middle of nowhere, and another in a busy university town with beautiful buildings and more great coffee shops than a girl could dream of.

I've also realised that it's fine to give my mum and dad a call, any time I like, for a chat about something I read, or to ask for advice, or to share my excitement about something someone just said to me in an email. I know there's nothing to prove in being aloof, or pretending I don't need help or feeling that maturity can only be reached by cutting myself off. That's just silly.

WHAT MAKES A FAMILY?

My family story is just one of many different formations and constructions of home life. I recognise the fact that I'm immensely fortunate with what I've got. But there are a dazzling number of different stories too, other compositions and dynamics and ways of growing up.

A possible list might include the following. Huge families. Only children. Kids close in age to their siblings. Then again, I have friends who have gaps of 15 years or more between them and their brothers and sisters. Some have cousins, while others, like me, have just the one – or none at all.

Many have divorced parents or a mother or father they don't know. Having stepparents or half brothers and sisters, families forged anew, is normal. So are single parents. So is that so-called nuclear family – mum, dad, two siblings – but a growing number have same-sex parents. Some kids have adopted parents, and some children are the parents, acting as a carer for their mum or dad. More young people than you'd imagine live with friends or extended family.

I could continue in this vein pretty much forever, talking about the distinctions between growing up in poverty or wealth, security or instability, in a situation filled with opportunities or enduring an utter lack of support. But perhaps the point is simply this: there are all sorts of sizes and situations when it comes to family – but it's the people within them who make and shape you.

Whatever your upbringing, one of the things that defines people is not just where they have come from, but what they do with it. People can kick hard against their upbringings, doing the absolute opposite to their parents, or stay in line with their family, voting for the same political parties or ending up doing almost identical jobs to their parents.

Most of the girls that I spoke to articulated very specific ways in which their upbringing influenced their own viewpoints and values. Asima, 17, who has three brothers and four sisters, said, *'I look up to my sisters. They're always there and are always kind to others. My religion has informed me too – I'm a Muslim – which means being kind, keeping respect and dignity, helping others and equality.'*

Willow, 16, who is home educated, told me of the *'open, direct, respectful relationship I have with my family (mostly my mum).'* She said, *'For me, how home education has affected my perspective goes hand in hand with how I was raised.'*

Others have a life that seems wonderful on the outside, but something still feels lacking. Louise, 26, was adopted as a child. She told me that, *'Because I came from Rwanda, with the history it had, many thought I was really lucky that I had a nice life, access to education, a nice house. Yet I spent my own life with an empty, black hole – like something had been taken away, but I didn't know what it was.'* She also discussed the challenges of growing up in a white family, which presented problems when it came to belonging and wanting to fit in, reflecting, *'People assume the "happy ever after" but it's not quite that straightforward.'*

If it seems like I've chosen three random examples there of family setups, you'd be pretty bang on. But I wanted to draw together a mere pinch of the many moments of insight and observation I gleaned from conversations about all these families, each seemingly unlike the other.

Although these particular young women had totally different backgrounds, they were more similar than they were different. Whether it was an interest in personal style, an amazing work ethic, or some pretty cool feminist sentiments, they were all influenced by what they'd grown up with, but developed interests and passions and attitudes beyond their families too.

We're such a mix of all the things around us: cultural messages, family values, friends' opinions, eye-opening books or something we find randomly online that totally transforms our understanding. Almost everything can have some bearing on how we see the world, and how we position ourselves within it.

Family is just a single strand within that mix of influences. Yet it's a particularly constant strand, a woven cord – one that should ideally bind you safely; be something you know you can always grab hold of if you need to.

PICKING FIGHTS AND SLAMMING DOORS

Unfortunately for the rest of the family, not to mention our door frames, my dad and I get wound up in the same way. From when I was about 13 to 15, this meant quite a few tears and slammed doors between us – and not always from my end.

Amusingly, my dad doesn't even remember this now, I had to gently remind him recently how we'd blow up at each other over silly things like doing the washing up, or the fallout if one of us made a snide comment. But we always made up quickly afterwards. With our hot tempers, the shouting was loud, but the reconciliation swift.

My door-slamming days are past. Now I very rarely fall out with my family. What changed between Dad and I to stop us arguing so much? Firstly, growing up. Hurdling through puberty and gaining a bit of emotional growth provides a toolkit to defuse the potential firecracker of a massive argument. Afraid that's not really a 'how to' – more of an 'it'll happen anyway'. But there are various things I've learnt since (even if I don't alwaaaaaays put them into practice).

THE ~~OFFICIAL UNITED NATIONS~~ GUIDE TO DEFUSING A FAMILY ARGUMENT

✳ Stay calm and listen. Most arguments start because people feel their viewpoint is being lost. If it can be explained without screeching, that's a great place to start.

✳ Ask if you can explain your own perspective, if it feels like you're not being listened to – and then do so calmly, rather than making accusations.

✳ Don't jump to conclusions. Giving people the benefit of the doubt can be helpful. If something they said sounded hurtful, ask them to explain why they said it.

✳ Try to avoid accusations altogether, especially of the 'you always …' variety. Describe exactly what you heard said without making a judgement. Then say how it makes you feel.

✳ Try not to push, push, push it. If you can see that there's a kind of explosive charge in the room, as tempting as it may be to see what happens if you provide the spark, it's usually easier to let it defuse. Take a deep breath. Back off.

✳ Respond, rather than react. This is something I try to apply all over the place. Reacting is that snap-second angry/irritated retort. Responding is more thoughtful and measured.

Also know that you can't change the way your siblings or parents respond to you, frustrating as that may be. You can only alter your own responses to them. This is the biggie. It applies throughout our lives: we can't change anyone else. We can only change ourselves.

 Learn when it's absolutely right to speak up and challenge your parents or siblings, and when holding that tongue might be a little more sensible, either because they may actually have a point too, or because you're both too upset to reach a compromise right now.

Sometimes it's easier to walk away. Do you want to be right, or happy? Fighting generally doesn't resolve stuff.

As much as I would have hated to hear this mid door-slamming rage, the 'I hate everyone, everything, and I'm running away/ locking myself in the bathroom/never speaking to you again' stuff is usually caused by a swirl of hormones, growing freedoms, and the often wobbly attempt to outline your own personality independently from your family.

Add in the influence of you and your peers running wild, the realisation that the world is a big and weird place that can be tough to navigate, and the creeping feeling that all your parents want to do is to embarrass you in front of friends – and it's not surprising that teens want to kick back.

One of my main faults is that I answer back – I can't help it. I know exactly what buttons to press, and I do feel guilty, but still …

Bea, 14 🔊

But, surprise, surprise, unless your parents have a particularly cruel sense of humour, they're not trying to intentionally embarrass you. They may not 'get' everything about what you're feeling and thinking about, but a lot of them do care enough to want to know. Give them a little credit for that. You may not see eye to eye on everything – it would be strange if you did – but they are usually doing their best, even if that does mean asking endless questions about exactly who you're going to be seeing on the weekends.

Also, parents aren't perfect. They are individuals who had lives before you – and have probably got drunk and done stupid stuff and have memories of adventures and places and jobs you might never find out that much about. But dig around a bit while you are chatting to them, and you may discover your parents are likely to be more understanding than you think about your own exploits. My parents are now incredibly open about their past, and I know a ton of stories about failed engagements, music festivals and the time my dad ran naked through a patch of nettles while hitchhiking across America (yeah, really).

It's easy to feel like no one else gets you or understands what you're going through, like parents or guardians are *just the worst* – full of endless rules and nagging and ways of stopping you having fun. In some cases, this is because parents are actually being overprotective and not giving you the space needed to grow up independently. But that will pass too. It will probably help to find out what they went through at your age.

Perhaps it's time to find out if they have some amazingly outrageous or intriguing skeletons in their closet. Failed exams, out of character instances of bravery, times when talking to a stranger yielded extraordinary things: or just simple stuff? Memories that still stick out. Moments they've carried with them. People they met. Places they went – whether it was a caravan by the sea or trekking through mountains.

Family stories, whether they're eccentric great-aunts, far-distant in-laws or just your own parents, are a rich seam to pick at – so many details and anecdotes and moments of real pathos. I particularly love finding out about my parents' pasts, as well as previous generations.

I know I'm fortunate in having a rather honest, open (perhaps sometimes a little too open) relationship with my folks. If yours are more of the mouth-shut, clammed-up variety, this might not work as well, although it's always worth trying. You never know what pinches of parental/grandparental wisdom they might reveal.

✱ What did they wear as young adults?

This is a reason to dig out old photos, and gives a simple, non-personal and fun way to start the conversation. What's more, it means you can either laugh at some of their fashion choices (my dad once had a suit that looked like it was made of sofa fabric), or admire their style – or perhaps both at the same time.

✱ What were their teen years like?

I've heard about my dad getting bullied horrendously at school, sticking glue in his hair when he decided 'punk' was the way forward. With my mum there's the enviable tales of her having access to jumble sales where genuine flapper dresses were 20p, her unorthodox upbringing and her adventures with friends throughout sixth form.

✱ What about previous boyfriends/girlfriends? Do they still remember much about them?

I actually found this both totally fascinating, and kind of helpful – especially because as a teen my dad was convinced he'd never end up in a relationship (where have I heard that before? Turn to page 197).

✱ What did previous generations of the family do for a living?

Although rags to riches may be the narrative favoured by Disney, even with less extreme tales you are guaranteed a few surprises. One of my great-grandmas was pretty remarkable for being a small-scale landlord at the point where women owning property was barely legal. On the other side of the family, my paternal great-grandfather was catapulted from being a successful businessman in Prague to refugee to janitor in Washington DC. That's quite a trajectory.

WHEN STUFF GETS TOUGH

Dealing with bereavement is a horrible, but inevitable, part of being alive. Most of us expect that it's something we'll only really have to deal with once we're adults. I'm lucky enough to have not experienced much direct loss beyond that of great-grandparents and grandparents, which – while extremely sad – wasn't unexpected, and felt (however much these things can feel like that) natural. We wrote poems for their funerals, cleared out their houses, commemorated their lives. It was tough, but not shocking.

Yet while I was putting together research for this book, other stories began to emerge. There was the girl who'd just lost a friend to an overdose. Another who talked about the impact of her dad dying just months before her GCSEs, explaining how her friends just didn't understand what she was trying to deal with – and that she couldn't speak to anyone about it other than her brother for ages. A third lost her best friend when she was ten, saying 'I'm upset on special days, like her birthday, death day and our "friendship day"... I go to the school she wanted to go to ... and so sometimes I feel guilty or bad for doing so.'

The stories from these teens all showed that the way in which one responds to loss varies. There is no set amount of time in which one is meant to move on, no single way to come to terms with it. Grieving is incredibly personal and intimate, full of variations and quirks, whether the one lost is a friend or family member. Some families are super-supportive, others struggle, either because they're shakily attempting to deal with it too, or because it's just beyond anything they're used to addressing. During times of instability though, a strong network can be truly invaluable.

That's why I've included thoughts about bereavement in this chapter. It's something that ruptures delicate connections and relationships – the ones assumed to be stable. Doesn't matter if it's someone you're related to by blood, or someone you chose because you relate to them so well.

Laura lost a friend. When I first heard her story, it felt like a punch in the stomach – a reminder of just how horrible and random things can be. She is only 18. Her words convey the experience so perfectly that I wanted to set them down here in their entirety.

Nothing on this earth can prepare you for the death of a friend. My darling friend Ben died unexpectedly of an exceptionally rare (and sadly undiagnosed) condition just weeks before we were both due to sit our first A-Level exam.

How my friends and I made it through those first few days I doubt I'll ever know. First, there was the spreading of the news – a task I wouldn't wish upon my worst enemy and yet one which had to be done.

The phone calls I made will stay with me forever. There was a deafening silence at the end of the line as each one of my friends was left speechless.

In the days that followed it was all we could do, as friends and classmates, to be together – simply sharing the weight of the tragedy. It's sad that sometimes it takes something so sorrowful to truly bring people together despite their differences, but the way we supported one another was remarkable.

Saying my last goodbye at Ben's funeral was the lowest point of my life. But despite my belief in the beginning that there was no escape from the tunnel of darkness I was trapped in – things are better. I know that somewhere, somehow, Ben is watching over me. His body might be gone, but his soul, and his spirit, are very much alive in those of us who knew and loved him.

WHEN FAMILIES AREN'T PERFECT

I watched my dad go through a terrible time, and it affected my whole family in different ways (see the next chapter for more on this). I've also seen some of my friends go through immensely troubling or tricky family situations requiring depths of strength, grace, and patience that I can only guess at. The realisation that bad things happen to good people can be a shocking life experience. And the worst thing about this random 'bad times' generator is that it definitely happens more to some people than others.

Being in a situation where responsibility and parent–child relationships become skewed is so hard. Parents or carers are meant to be predictable, safe, secure. Behaviour that is unexpected, embarrassing or shaming, or just plain scary, making you feel out of control and abandoned, shouldn't be on the cards. But just because it *shouldn't*, doesn't mean it isn't going to crop up.

Although there are so many wonderful, stable families out there, if you're part of one of them, don't forget how lucky you are. Growing up safe in the knowledge that the key adults around you care for you, love you, and can be there for you, is one of the biggest benefits you can be given.

In the natural course of talking to people for the research on this book, so many stories were thrown up – of bereavement, divorce, adoption, being a young carer, of parents suffering from alcoholism or mental health problems, and of teens feeling afraid to take friends home. And although those may sound like situations more suited to true-life tales or posters in school corridors, they're just plain reality for too many young people, who have no choice but to get on with what comes their way – no matter how bad things get. There are all sorts of shades and depths to trouble, temporary experiences and ongoing problems; things that are easily resolved and plenty of others that are incredibly hard to even talk about.

One group of teens that doesn't get nearly enough recognition or support is the group of people who find themselves playing an unusual role in family life: that of caregiver. These young people are often forgotten by their peers and by society at large. I got chatting to Stella, whose mum was diagnosed with Alzheimers when she was 50, and Stella was 17. Now at 19, Stella's one of her primary carers. She very kindly agreed to explain some of the things she has to do to care for her mum.

One of the main challenges Stella talked about is how her mum has to be assisted in simple tasks like getting dressed. *'Buttons, zips, buckles and ties are all impossible for her,'* she says, *'and we've bought clothes easy for her to deal with herself but they'll often be inside out or back to front if you don't help her.'*

It's not just the practical bits like reminding her mum how to hold knives and forks either. *'Her short-term memory is reduced,'* Stella points out, *'so she'll ask you the same question over and over ... Her attention span is short and she forgets the details of the story she might be trying to tell, so I fill in lots of gaps in facts, details and names.'* Her mum's condition also means that her mood can change from upbeat to angry or frustrated very quickly.

The thing that unites a lot of young carers is the lack of recognition from friends (and sometimes teachers). Stella continues, *'I think I feel distanced from a lot of my contemporaries because we have completely different priorities.'* She told very few people at her sixth form, and even those friends who did know about her mum weren't always the most understanding about why she might be late, or have to leave things early. Stella said, '*They would question why I wasn't making enough effort to see them.*'

It's awful if your peers are talking about snazzy holidays they've been on, or the wonderful time they had with family on the weekend, or even just complaining about their mum who you know is a perfectly lovely woman, while you're simply trying to cope with each day as it comes. It's crap. We shouldn't pretend it isn't. So what can be done when people – you or your friends – are facing a difficult challenge?

Whether you are the friend standing by to offer support or you are struggling through a difficult time yourself, it's so important to remember that *you* matter. *You matter so very much.* Your feelings and experiences are important, even if they don't seem to be recognised by others.

When you find yourself feeling completely alone or in the middle of a warzone, always remember your family problems are never your fault or responsibility. On the other hand, you do have a personal debt to yourself. Viewing yourself as someone worth treating well is always your number one priority and responsibility.

Taking care of yourself in times of need is entirely necessary, more so than at other times, don't let anyone suggest otherwise. What taking care of yourself involves is up to you, there's no one size fits all guide to care, but it probably means:

Don't bottle up your emotions
Allowing yourself to feel whatever comes your way (anger, upset, bone-aching tiredness, frustration)

Escape when you can

Working on ways to escape for a while (being creative, seeing friends, finding an interest that is yours and yours alone)

Plan your time

Dealing with any problems practically (asking for help, planning ahead on what you have to complete by the end of each week)

Don't try to be a superhero – you already are

Just knowing that it's ok to admit that some days it's all a bit too much.

The teens I spoke to for help with this section all emphasised how great it was finding a solid support group. It could be one specifically devoted to what you've experienced (for example, a young carers' group). On the other hand, your support group might just be a selection of people close to you, who get what you are dealing with: extended family, good friends, and others who can listen – not forgetting any of the heroes who make you the odd meal or are just generally lovely. Online communities can be excellent too. Your support group, however it's formed, should give you a space to talk, to put into words what's going on. Finding support is about knowing that are so many people out there who *do* care about your wellbeing, who are on your side, who know what you are going through and who know just how great you are.

FINDING A SURROGATE FAMILY

For ages, my mum had a postcard up in our kitchen with a picture of four jolly-looking ladies on it, with a caption saying 'Friends are God's apology for relatives'. It was particularly pertinent at that point, as my mum found herself looking after various elderly relatives. Much of each week was taken up with shopping, lengthy phone conversations, arranging medical appointments and liaising with carers. Her friends provided some relief – people she could laugh with and talk to, who were removed from the situations she was dealing with.

I still love the sentiment behind that postcard, especially because friends might not always be an 'apology', but they're certainly an addition. As I've mentioned before, in my own family setup we've created honorary family members thanks to the lack of actual ones (due in part to my mum being the only child of two only children and my dad being left an only child after his brother's death). I've even found myself a set of 'fairy' godparents – based on the *Cinderella* idea of a lovely someone who unexpectedly offers treats or support. These friends of my parents did everything I could wish for, from introducing me to interesting books to helping to support our family through some incredibly tough times – especially my spinal surgery, and my dad's severe depression. In both instances they were on hand to provide company, food and practical help. We're very lucky to have them, as well as our other friends who are regarded as surrogate siblings or cousins.

There are other types of 'family' to be found too. One of the more exciting things about making your own way in the world is the ability to build a community of your own: a handful of people who you can ring in the middle of the night if you absolutely need someone to talk to.

They may not be family in the same way as your own folks – they can be either more or less important, depending on what your home life is like. But they are something new, and chosen exclusively by you. There'll be challenges and difficulties there too, but also new opportunities and experiences you possibly wouldn't get to on your own.

Not everyone creates a picture-perfect home-away-from-home at uni or elsewhere, but you are sure to meet some interesting people as your world expands. I think I've created a family of sorts for myself, but it's made up of scattered individuals, rather than a core group, maybe because my own family is so small.

Now more and more teens get to develop communities before they even leave home, with online spaces providing support, shared interests and more. Whether you're interested in gaming, reading, LGBTQ rights, vlogging, feminism, maths, politics, or films, there'll be something out there.

So if you don't get on with your own family? Make your own. Seek out people. Be interested in other people, remain open to opportunities. And if you do get on with everyone in your family, then at least you can add some other significant figures into the mix.

WHAT'S INSIDE YOUR HEAD?

5

STAYING HEALTHY ON THE INSIDE

We get a lot of advice about how to stay healthy. I bet most of us could whip up some top tips about keeping our bodies happy and functioning. But what about mental health?

General mental wellbeing can be influenced by physical factors too: exercise and sleep don't just help your body recharge, they are also great for your mind. And just like problems your physical body can have – anything from a slightly dodgy knee from that epic fall you took in netball to a sudden, shocking, and extremely messy nosebleed in the middle of an exam – your mental health can have various shades of wellness and unwellness. Some mental health problems are quite huge and scary, others are easy to fix. Some come out of nowhere, others are brought on by particularly trying or traumatic circumstances. Some come and go quite quickly, others need long-term care.

WHY WORDS MATTER

My experience with mental health had quite an extreme start (see page 154). My dad suddenly had to be admitted to a psychiatric unit for severe depression, a traumatic experience for him – and the rest of the family.

Before he got ill, I definitely used the word 'depressed' where I meant 'actually quite pissed off'. Mental health terms are used all the time in everyday conversation, often with completely twisted meanings. Comments such as 'it's so *depressing* our exam's tomorrow', or 'she went totally *schiz*', or 'I'm a bit *OCD* about cleaning my room' are pretty common, and each one of these references a mental health term which bears little resemblance to the kinds of behaviour or event we are referring to. But it's really important to realise that every time we use one of these words the wrong way, we start to muddy the true meaning as well.

After a while, a term like 'OCD' becomes confused with the desire to line up objects on a table or obsessively clean the house. For some, that might be one example among other outward symptoms of this anxiety disorder – accompanied by unstoppable, awful thoughts, and moments of total panic. For others, it has little to do with organisation. Regardless, OCD is usually exhausting in the ways it affects a person's day-to-day life. Reducing a term for something serious to an adjective to describe oddball behaviour (or just a desire to put things in colour order) devalues the true nature of this condition.

WHY THE BIG TABOO?

Mild mental health problems like stress are very common. So why is it that people are happy to come into school after a break and announce they've been off with the flu but not that they have got anxiety or another equally common mental health problem? Part of the issue is that it's much more difficult to talk about an illness when you can't see the effects. Broken legs are easily seen, and it's easy to support someone who has a broken leg: it's obvious what they need help with. But there are no bandages or casts for the mind – and much less in the way of flowers, gifts or 'Sorry you're ill' cards.

This issue of not being able to see problems makes them much more mysterious, too. Although the words surrounding a condition might be well known, as we have noted above, the condition itself is often misunderstood – treated with a fear and shame not attached to physical illnesses.

One of the main problems with mental health is the stigma and silence. It's time we started talking openly about these common experiences: if we get used to discussing them, they won't be nearly so weird or scary sounding.

People are scared of mental health because of the word 'mental'. I avoid the topic and try to make out I'm fine, when all I really need is for someone to understand.

Orli, 14 📢

To me, it is extraordinary that although one in five teens experience mental health problems, teaching young people about mental health is virtually ignored in school classrooms. Let that sink in. Potentially 20 per cent of students will at some time suffer from a mental health problem, but there is no formal education in UK schools to help us understand what that might be like, or how to deal with it. Amy, 14, told me that she wished lessons could tell others that there's more to mental health than stereotypes. Similarly, Louise, 26, said she'd have loved it if '*the message that it's ok not to be ok*' had been emphasised in school.

However, there is now an increasing pressure for mental health to be taught. A fledgling, fluttering little hope of mine is that by the time this book comes out, these calls will be even louder and even more likely to translate into action. Conversation is a vital tool in challenging ignorance.

WHERE TO FIND OUT MORE

If you would like to learn more about mental health, these are some excellent places to start (for a more urgent matter, you'll find more info on page 150):

- **Mind** is *the* mental health charity and their website has tons of information including treatment options, how to get support and what it might be, even your legal rights and some help with supporting others. **www.mind.org.uk**

- **Young Minds** have lots of information aimed directly at young people about how to improve your mental health, types of mental illness that are common, understanding treatments and links to other organisations

that might be helpful, as well as information for parents, if needed.
www.youngminds.org.uk

❋ **Student Minds** is also a great place to go if you are away at college
or uni. It has stuff aimed at the student population – who can have just
the same problems as everyone else – but it also has advice for things
directly related to being a student such as the dreaded exam stress.
www.studentminds.org.uk

❋ **The World Health Organisation** has been involved in the production
of two YouTube videos that give a sense of what it's like to live with
depression, and how friends, partners or family members can help.
www.youtube.com/watch?v=XiCrniLQGYc and **www.youtube.
com/watch?v=2VRRx7Mtep8**

❋ **CAMHS (Child and Adolescent Mental Health Services)** offer
support through a range of services, and have been a lifeline to
many. Whatever is going on with you, there's someone out there
who can help. They won't be shocked, and they won't judge. The NHS
outlines what they do here. **http://www.nhs.uk/NHSEngland/
AboutNHSservices/mental-health-services-explained/Pages/
camhs-information-for-children-and-young-people.aspx**

❋ **Just interested?** To find out more about mental health campaigns,
research and support, go to the Mental Health Foundation website.
They don't provide direct help and support but their website has links to
many organisations that do. **www.mentalhealth.org.uk**
You can also find all of these helpful websites via Facebook and Twitter.

THE DAY THINGS CHANGED

My dad was diagnosed with severe clinical depression when I was in my first year of sixth form. I later found out that one in four people will suffer from a mental health issue in their lifetime. But back then I was almost totally unaware of what depression actually meant.

With my dad, I knew he'd had problems before. But those had been in his teens and 20s – a different life as far as I was concerned. The revelation that he was depressed in his mid-40s was a real shock. He'd been having trouble sleeping – but my dad was always complaining about his insomnia and back pain, so we'd all thought he was just suffering from his usual problems.

He hid it well at first, protecting us. But when I was 16 his depression hit a point where concealment was no longer possible. My memory of being told is sketched in bold lines. An autumn evening, me sitting in my bedroom typing up an essay. My mum knocked on the door and asked if she and Dad could come in. They sat on my bed. Mum said, 'Roz, we have something to tell you.' The first thought that flickered up was 'Shit – they're getting divorced.' By comparison, being told my dad was going into a psychiatric unit for a while felt like a welcome relief, at least in the first few seconds. Then the questions began. Why had we not known there was a problem earlier? How bad was it? Why did he have to go away? My brother was called in and given the news. He asked whether he was allowed to swear, and a surreal window followed, with us all laughing as he swore with great pleasure.

Laughter was in short supply after that point. Our house, lacking Dad's schoolboy giggles and rude jokes, felt too empty, too quiet. He came home to visit one weekend, but was rushed back after an episode of psychosis. (Psychosis is when someone perceives or interprets things differently from those around them, including having hallucinations or delusions.) After he was gone, we were surrounded again by more emptiness, more quiet.

A month or so later we drove to see him, chilly November mists horribly fitting as I tried to talk to a man with a fogged-up mind. I say 'a man' for a reason. During the time he was ill, this tall figure looked like my dad – but it wasn't him. He had my dad's height and face, but none of his life. This man's hands shook, his shoulders were hunched, his lack of conversation all too noticeable. My dad had been hollowed out.

After two months he came home again. In truth, this was worse. When he was away, I could disconnect, treat it like a long business trip or holiday he'd eventually return from. Having him sit day after day on the sofa in the living room, I was faced by his empty eyes, and inability to respond to anything I said. His presence was a constant reminder of just how altered life had become. The house was physically stuffy and hot, because Dad was so convinced of the cold he'd turned the heating up high enough for the downstairs to become a tropical cave. When I was out I'd get countless calls from him as he worried about my whereabouts. When I was in the house, I wanted to hide from the figure on the sofa – or perhaps scream at him.

I now know my anger wasn't really directed at him, but at his illness. Yet during those months it was almost impossible to tell where my dad ended and the depression began. Although I had a very faint grasp of what he was going through and how he was feeling, this didn't stop my desire to shout at him to stop it, to come back, to recover. I wanted my dad back! Of course he couldn't just snap out of it. Dad wanted to recover and come back to us desperately, but at that time it was a life raft just beyond his reach.

I was fortunate enough to have one stable parent throughout the whole experience – my wonderful mum. She is incredible. My spine may be literally lined with metal, but hers is metaphorically much stronger. During those six months she took on new roles, still mother to us, and wife to Dad – but also carer. She made my brother's packed lunch for school, picked me up from the train after college and made sure she spent time with us both, all the while looking after Dad – making him do the evening cooking, keeping the house in order, picking up his medication, taking him for appointments, just keeping a constant, patient eye on him. Her only time off came when close friends took over, lifting the weight of responsibility for an hour or two. I'll always value the time she took to talk to my brother and me, explaining and helping us to gain a tiny glimpse of what our dad was feeling (or not feeling).

It's hard to explain what depression *is*. I'm no expert, but I've tried to read up on it since, to understand what he went through. For people who have mild depression the symptoms and resulting changes in mood and behaviour are much less severe than what my dad went through – perhaps just a feeling of detachment or disinterest, as if you are viewing the world through a bubble, unable to really connect with anyone or anything. Depression can be identified by feelings of worthlessness, guilt, self-hatred, or even a kind of nothingness. In more extreme cases, it can be seen in an inability to get out of bed or communicate, and can create a state in which even the most normal of activities are impossible. For some the psychological pain is so extreme that they feel like they'd do anything to escape it.

Luckily, my mum was there to talk us through the possible triggers for Dad's depression, and encouraged us all to think that, although it felt impossible to imagine, we *had* to believe his depression would lift and he'd return.

He did. It took time, and a pattern of two-steps-forward-and-one-step-back as he seemingly got better and then returned to the sofa once more. It took plenty of hopeful little signs – the first time he was willing to come out for a walk, or the attempt at making a (terrible) joke. The days when he responded to conversation were greeted with relief, the ones where he was silent all the worse when we'd seen a glimpse of our old dad again. But as the months rolled on he came back to us. Medication, cognitive behavioural therapy and counselling helped his recovery.

When my dad was just recovering, I went on an week-long English literature residential course. I shared a train journey back with another girl who had been on the same course. We hadn't really talked all week, and yet found ourselves having an incredibly intense conversation that stretched on hour after hour. The topic? One mention of my dad and we were off. She had been through bouts of depression herself.

I can't really remember what we said now, but still recall the crackle of that shared connection – the relief for both of us, in our very different positions, of having someone to talk to, at last. Someone who knew more about mental health, or mental ill health, than anyone else ever had. She's now a very dear friend.

DO YOU THINK YOU MIGHT WANT SOME HELP?

If you are struggling and want to talk to someone, your local GP (family doctor) can be super-helpful. Your family is probably already registered with a GP, and you don't need to take your parents with you if you don't want to. It can be difficult to know what to say so DocReady is a simple program that helps you to identify what you want to tell your doctor and gives you a checklist so that you remember when you go in (**www.docready. org**). If you are living away from home you can register with a GP near your accommodation. On the other hand, there are loads of places to get help without going to the doctor or asking at school.

Relate have a children and young people's counselling service where you can see someone at your local Relate centre. You can also have a free live chat session or talk on the phone about any concerns via their website (**www.relate.org.uk**).

ChildLine is another fab confidential service for anyone under 19: you can talk to a trained person about anything you want to. Their website has lots of useful information too and you can have a live chat or send them an email if you like. **www.childline.org.uk**, or just call free on 0800 1111.

Samaritans are available to talk to anytime, about anything bothering you (they emphasise you don't have to be suicidal to call them). **www.samaritans.org** or call 08457 90 90 90.

I NEED HELP, NOW, DAMMIT!

If you are feeling too ill to fanny around on the internet, or you are starting to feel desperate or in urgent need of help or support, the places below are available 24 hours a day and can help you immediately.

* **Samaritans:** Call 08457 90 90 90
* **ChildLine:** Call 0800 1111
* **NHS 111** (An instant health helpline in England & Wales): Dial 111
* **NHS 24** (The same thing but in Scotland): Call 08454 242424
* You can also contact your GP surgery or their out of hours service
* Or simply take a taxi to your nearest A&E, or call 999.

If you are not sure what to say, don't worry about it: just make the first step and the professionals will help you explain what you are going through. All these guys exist to help *you*.

EATING DISORDERS

Although they can have very damaging (though not always visible) physical effects, eating disorders are a mental health problem, and are common to varying degrees in teens and young people. Something that shocked me slightly during the interviews I carried out to research this book was just how many of the teens I spoke to said, 'Yeah I can discuss eating disorders – I've been through that/my friend has been there.' Each person had their own tale to tell, their own set of circumstances and reasons and ways of coping.

Georgina, 18, has worked through health-related anxiety and depression, as well as an eating disorder, which she describes as follows.

> I think anorexia's something that nobody really understands, and that people treat as a kind of flippant thing ... I was in a hospital for ten days. It was disgusting. I hated it. Not eating takes its toll so dramatically on you. I was admitted because I couldn't go to the loo any more – my body had shut down. It felt like the most horrible, humiliating thing.
>
> I was so tiny that sitting down hurt, lying down hurt, walking hurt. When I walked I could feel the bones in my feet. That's the ugly side. I was deficient in every kind of nutrient possible.

At that time I'd never wanted to be anything other than skinny and very fit – which meant that I couldn't concentrate on other things. I was so frenetic about it that everything went wrong. Obsession was the only way I felt like I could tidy my life up. That's the best way to describe it. I could put everything in one box with the anorexia. I felt like my life was on hold.

In recent years, the largest rise in admissions to hospital for eating disorders has been among those aged 10 to 19 – with the most common age for young women being 15, and for young men 13. Statistics like this only cover those who end up hospitalised. Actual numbers will always remain hidden. Listen to anyone talking about what they've been through with an eating disorder – how life-consuming it is, how exhausting, how hard it is to escape – and the cost is clear.

The NHS says that eating disorders are characterised by an abnormal attitude towards food that causes someone to change their eating habits and behaviour. Causes can be very complex, affected by anything from difficult experiences to biological history to a concern about being slim, or excessive focus on a person's weight, to being caused by other mental health problems or accompanying stressful situations.

One of the biggest dangers of eating disorders is that they are so misunderstood and underestimated. You don't have to look ill to be ill. It's affecting an increasing number of guys. Anorexia actually only makes up 10 per cent of eating disorders – with bulimia, binge-eating and EDNOS (Eating Disorder

Not Otherwise Specified) less well-acknowledged, although potentially just as damaging. There's also a spectrum from food restriction and calorie counting through to starvation.

Poppy, 19, wrote to tell me about her bulimia, and the negative effect body image issues can have on young teens.

I was kind of fat when I was younger, not huge but bigger than my peers. Once I realised that I was appalled. It seemed like the worst thing ever. I remember sitting in primary school and being disgusted at how fat my forearms looked resting on the table. It makes me sad for little me, you know? I wish I could give her a hug and tell her it doesn't matter.

My best friend and I used to diet together, and as we got older it got more and more out of hand; I ended up in a vicious binge/purge cycle of bulimia. Looking back the scariest thing is how much I normalised it in my own head. I figured everybody struggles with something and this was my 'thing'. I was making myself really ill, not to mention seriously unhappy and I didn't see anything wrong with it. I was depressed and missing school because I couldn't deal with leaving the house and facing up to normal responsibilities – it all felt overwhelmingly stressful.

Eventually I got called out by a teacher for missing lessons and told her about what was happening.

I started seeing the school counsellor, who was amazing, and working through my issues with food.

It's no way to live your life, crying at a plate of fish fingers, and it makes me angry seeing how ingrained dieting is for so many women. We don't talk about health or nutrition; it's always about weight loss. The language we use is so negative, the way magazines describe clothes as 'hiding' or 'disguising' parts of you – it heavily implies there's something wrong with those parts. It shouldn't be normal to hate yourself, or for what you ate at lunch to dictate your happiness.

If you think you have problems with food or want to know more about eating disorders, there are plenty of avenues for help.
Beat – Beating Eating Disorders – is the UK's leading charity and go-to place for anyone affected by eating disorders or difficulties with food, weight and shape. The website has helplines, support groups and information about finding treatment. Go to **www.b-eat.co.uk**. They even have a special service for anyone under 25. You can call 0345 634 7650 or email **fyp@b-eat.co.uk** or text 07786 20 18 20. You will also find information about eating problems on the websites of **Mind**, **Young Minds**, **Student Minds** and the **Mental Health Foundation** (see pages 143–4 for details).

THE PROBLEM OF SELF-HARM

Some mental health problems can be recognisably physical – something that is going on inside your head can present with very clear outward signs. One example of this is self-harming. If you are causing physical damage to yourself, always seek help. If you suspect, or are certain, that someone you know may be causing harm to themselves, again, seek help. This is serious, and needs to be treated seriously. It's important to recognise what is going on, act fast and get appropriate support. Contact any of the organisations and charities mentioned in this chapter for immediate help, or talk to your school or GP.

WATCH WHAT YOU ARE LOOKING AT

The internet is generally fantastic, and can be a great support for people with mental health problems, offering support groups and professional advice, not to mention lots of lovely distractions. But it can also be a very dark place, in particular for people with eating disorders. There are actually some sites out there that encourage things to spiral further. I want to keep this brief, because the less attention such sites get, the better.

It happens for other mental illnesses too. Websites glamorise self-harm and suicide, making them seem desirable rather than damaging, normalising traumatic or harmful actions. And in their normality, they're incredibly dangerous.

WHY IS MENTAL HEALTH PORTRAYED IN SUCH A MESSED-UP WAY?

Maybe part of the reason for such a high volume of content available online seeming to celebrate poor mental health is the enduring belief that it is somehow cool.

> It has become so fashionable recently to 'be depressed'. It's really annoying. Sitting in a counsellor's office and wanting to leave class and having panic attacks and feeling awful – people romanticise it, but it's really shitty.
>
> Amy, 14

It reminds me of an image that crops up again and again in popular culture: the messed-up but captivating young woman. She's 'crazy' enough to do worrying, impulsive things – but not to stop looking gorgeous. Her melancholy makes her fascinating. She's a lovely, broken eccentric and ready to have her life transformed. Someone just needs to step in and make her *better*. Think of the TV programmes that only show very ill girls if they are also incredibly attractive; or YA books where young women just pine after boys and rarely eat. Whatever her particular form, she crops up again and again.

This isn't to dismiss anyone whose experiences resemble the examples above, or who has found solace in those kinds of stories. But it still feels wrong for there to be so many examples where mental health is an interesting facet to a personality – rather than something to be sensitively explored. Too often mental ill health is presented as cool and kooky, not horrible.

Do you know what's not cool? Weird dreams thanks to the side effects of antidepressants, or a hyper-manic state where concentrating is difficult when you have a deadline to meet. It's not fun to feel out of control thanks to a panic attack, it's not ok to damage your physical health due to lack of nutrition – and it's as far away from cool as you can get to feel so full of self-hatred that a harmful way out seems like a good idea.

ACE YA BOOKS THAT TALK MENTAL HEALTH

More and more authors are working to depict mental health with nuance and balance - not to mention cool heroines you will fall instantly in love with.

- **Fangirl** by Rainbow Rowell – A light approach to talking about social anxiety and other mental health problems.
- **Finding a Voice** by Kim Hood – A story of friendship between a girl who acts as carer for her mum and a boy with cerebral palsy.
- **All the Bright Places** by Jennifer Niven – A boy-meets-girl story with a frank approach to mental illness and suicide.
- **Am I Normal Yet?** by Holly Bourne – A relatable, honest read exploring the effects of OCD that will resonate with everyone.
- **Lottie Biggs is (Not) Mad** by Hayley Long – Funny, relatable and warm, Long's book takes a more serious twist as the protagonist realises she's dealing with some potentially significant mental health problems.
- **Wintergirls** by Laurie Halse Anderson – A powerful and sometimes painful depiction of eating disorders.

YES, I'M STRESSED!

When we talk about mental health, it tends to be when that 'health' part has tipped over into the not-so-healthy. But just like our physical wellness, the other side to being unwell is, where possible, looking at ways to maintain our mental wellbeing. (And, brilliantly, there's even an equivalent of getting your '5 a day' for your mind. See here for more info: http://www.fivewaystowellbeing.org)

There've been points in my life of high stress – of bloody tough stuff to navigate. Sometimes things seemed almost unmanageable. There were the standard hoops to jump through like exams and university applications and frantic attempts to stay afloat with work, but also 'big life' moments like recovering from spinal surgery, seeing my dad's depression, and subsequently responding to a close friend's mental health problems. During all of these episodes, I struggled at times. There were moments where I didn't know if I could continue – where the overwhelming difficulties or raw, throbbing pain felt too huge to manage. But, in fact, it's easier to cope than not cope.

Routine is helpful. I like giving structure to my hours. I try to get on with what is required of me, breaking it all down into manageable chunks, which was as useful when I was literally learning to walk again as when I was trying to hit all my deadlines during my GCSEs. Same principle, whether it's a physical challenge to overcome or a mental problem. I attempt to take it all a day at a time. For me, dealing with stressful situations is about facing what is in front of me, rather than projecting what might happen in the future.

Talking it through with others is a godsend too. When I was panicking over A-Levels, I went and chatted to my history teacher in advance. I just needed some reassurance. When my best friend's anxiety and depression started, it had a terrible effect on me too, and it took me far too long to realise that I was in trouble as well. She was sick, but I really started to struggle too, under the pressure (that I mainly put on myself) to look after her. Her illness also meant a gap opened up in my life. The space usually filled with silly messages and late-night chats suddenly emptied. But once I realised I needed help, I made sure to discuss how I was feeling with my parents, getting a helpful outside perspective from them. Family and friends are the ones who continue to support me when I'm feeling lonely, or frustrated or achingly sad.

A problem shared is not necessarily a problem halved, but it's guaranteed to be a little lighter. For a long time I was much too good at being tight-lipped, my pride not allowing me to reveal my fragility to others. I wanted to be the strong one who had it all sorted. But then I realised that part of having it sorted is also being honest about your emotions, knowing when you can push on, and when you really, really need someone else to be there for you – whether that's a mate you can sob on the phone to or a professional who might be able to shed a bit of light and guidance moving forwards.

WHAT WILL GET YOU THROUGH IT?

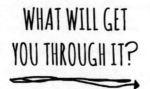

It's not always the solution to life's problems to have a good cry, but my chief method of dealing with stress involves a more-than-occasional bout of weeping. The sense after a good cry, for me, is similar to the smell of grass after rainfall – everything is cleared out, hopefully a little refreshed. The storm has subsided to a grumble. I have friends who rarely cry, and prefer quiet practicality to the odd outburst. Depends on your style. And perhaps the local supply of tissues.

Of course this and the following advice only works in situations where you can realistically hope to make changes by yourself. It's a tough balance trying to give useful tips for mental wellbeing. These things work for odd days of feeling a bit poo, rather than for tackling bigger problems. In those situations, saying 'pull yourself together' or 'just put a smile on your face' would be the crappest, least feeling thing in the world. If you can't actually get up out of bed for physical or mental reasons, you can't get up – and you shouldn't feel bad about it.

That said, there are basic wellness targets to hit when you are feeling under the weather. Sometimes these are so obvious that we forget about them in times of stress. I'm talking the most simple cornerstones of everyday living – eating enough, keeping hydrated, getting enough sleep, working out your frustration in exercise and giving over some time and space to look after yourself. When you're hungry, thirsty, tired, sluggish and feeling a bit stressy, it's even more infuriating to attempt, well, anything. Trying to socialise with me when I'm knackered and starving is not a good idea, as I'm sure many of my friends would happily confirm …

If you have run down the basic checklist and are fed and watered and still feeling wound-up or overwhelmed, I can recommend one of two routes. The first involves action. Anything from taking a shower to going swimming to having a fast-paced cycle that leaves me breathless. I'm also a big fan of angry, long stomps – parks, woods and lengths of pavement all work.

The second involves retreat. I take to bed for a stint of crap movies, return to my favourite childhood books that feel ever so safe – the Moomins, oh the Moomins, they got me through some tough weeks after surgery – sketch, scrapbook, snooze and listen to music. Others I chatted with mentioned everything from mindfulness colouring books to cooking as their go-to activities. Whatever gives *you* the right dose of respite and lets your mind reset.

Then, when I need to get up, and find myself still feeling like shit, it's time for the make-up bag to work its small acts of magic. I get up, put on a dress I know I look bloody great in, add eyeliner, perfume and lashings of bright red lipstick. I perform the assurance I'm not necessarily feeling. Sometimes it's enough to lift me back into a fleeting state of normality and just get me out of the door, ready to face the world.

THE ALL-TIME GREATEST 'I FEEL LIKE SHIT' BUSTERS ✎⟶

Throughout all the tough times I have experienced, I have learned to remind myself of several things, either by writing these thoughts down on a piece of paper or by simply taking a moment to say them inside my head:

✻ **1) I am not in a box.**

I do not have to be defined by any of the following: my achievements, my grades, my exam results, my inbox, my waistline, my work, my relationship status or the way people view me or think of me.

✻ **2) This too – whatever 'this' is – shall pass.**

However bad it seems, it won't be like that forever. Lives, feelings, health and thousands of other things shift and move on. To borrow a line my dad likes to repeat all the time: 'the only constant is change'.

✻ **3) Regardless of what's going on, I am still a valuable person.**

I deserve to be cared about, and shall always strive to care about others.

✻ **4) I have a lot of things in my life to be grateful for.**

A while back I went through a phase of listing them, from the biggest ('I am loved') to the most particular ('my hair is looking great today'). This is a way of reminding myself of everything I have, rather than focusing what I lack or see as a shortcoming.

✻ **5) It's never too late to start your day again.**

That's another favourite family motto. Starting your day again is the equivalent of flipping a mental 'reboot' switch. It's a decision to shake off the big, grey, glowering cloud of grump, irritation, anger or panic, and make like you actually got out of bed on the right side that morning.

WE'RE ONLY HUMAN

Like most of us, I'm not perfect at following my own advice. And that's ok. All of these different ideas for dealing with the tough stuff are about prioritising yourself, and part of that is about not feeling guilty when coping isn't quite possible.

Of course, there's also the possibility that some areas of stress and anxiety are beyond your control to help. Maybe that means you need to look at your lifestyle to see what's causing the problems (are you burning the candle at both ends? Have you got beyond the stage where a few weekends of really hard work will help you catch up with your homework? Is someone in particular causing you a problem?).

If I had no experience of the darker side of mental health problems, I could finish here with some nice, sickly-sweet phrase about difficult times making us stronger. But when you're finding it all a muddle or a mess, the last thing you want is platitudes.

What you are feeling may require something else too, like talking to your school or college, your doctor or another local advisor about a course of counselling or some other gentle therapy like mindfulness or meditation. If some 'thing' is getting in the way of you being you, it's time to talk it over with someone who can help. That's ok. All of those things – therapies, mental exercises, meditation courses, medications – exist to help make your existence a little easier and rewarding.

FRIENDSHIPS
& FITTING IN

6

FRIENDS MAKE EVERYTHING BETTER

When I was little, one of my best friends lived in the middle of nowhere, her house the only sign of life for several miles around. It looked like someone had just plonked it down at the bottom of a valley, hemmed in on all sides by woods. Her mum gave us tons of freedom, and whenever I visited we'd spend our days roaming the countryside: wading up the stream, making fires, building dens, turning bushes into spaceships or climbing to the top of a nearby slope where a swing hung from a tree. We'd kick out on the swing and swoop above the hill, the house, the wood-smoke. The only other person we could see was the small figure of her mum doing the gardening below.

When my friend moved, we lost touch, but I treasure the memory of our escapades. We'd return in the evening muddy, damp and a bit grotty, but jubilant. Although none of my current friendships are as outdoorsy, I think traces of those early years remain in the people I seek out as friends. I appreciate playfulness, chattiness, huge imaginations and a willingness to get stuck in.

Relationships come and go but your friends are constant. Friends are where you head when you need someone to shed tears on, a sofa to sink into and watch movies, a partner in crime: they are always there to share your narrow escapes, for all-night conversations, creative endeavours, secrets shared, support in tough times, sleepovers, trips and train journeys. Friends are for dressing up, hanging around outside in summer, exploring your town and going further afield. They are for parties, cooking experimental foods, music festivals, first time experiences, 3am fits of laughter and a deep-rooted sense of support and trust – of being there for one another. My best friend and I have decided that if, come 50, neither of us have partners, then we will marry, live a glamorous existence and adopt a litter of kittens. We've already mooted the possibility of buying a houseboat too.

I love my range of friends now, but my early teen years weren't great for friendships. I value the amazing people I have in my life all the more because I used to feel so insecure and uncertain about where – if anywhere – I fitted in. Some people adore school, forming life-long friendships there. I was not one of them. The status games and social rankings wore away at my self-esteem – to the point where I usually came home feeling miserable. I was relieved to finally escape, moving to a new school for sixth form.

My social life is almost unrecognisable these days, by comparison. I have given concern about where I fit in conventional social ranking the boot, and the people I count as good friends range from girls several years younger than me to women in their 50s and beyond. I've kept in contact with a few close friends from school and sixth form – a small but select bunch who've all moved off in disparate, interesting ways – and have made plenty of new mates at university. We've bonded over spoken-word poetry, cooked big breakfasts in our teeny student kitchens and huddled together for windswept chats during breaks outside the library.

I've got to know lots of new faces through writing and work – and several from life online too. One wonderful friend appeared in a magazine feature on up-and-coming teens that I also took part in; another was a fellow model at *The Observer* Ethical Awards. There's a fabulous photographer who wanted to take photos of my scoliosis surgery scars, and a make-up artist (one of the warmest and most generous women ever) who read something I'd written on body image and then we had a chance meeting at a party.

I love meeting new people, warmed by that first crackle of questions and debate and laughter. Sometimes you will end up chatting with someone where you quickly realise there's little there for either of you, but it's always worth taking the risk.

For me, the best friendships are the ones where there's an ease of talking and exchanging stories without the worry of judgement, but with people who are willing to challenge you. Someone who will apologise when they mess up, or accept your apology when you do. The buddies who, when you're feeling fragile, will come curl up with you or drag you out for a day of distractions. It's the beautiful simplicity of being entirely comfortable in their presence. You have nothing to prove to each other.

My best friend is really trustworthy – I tell her things and I'm not worried that she'll tell anyone else. I can be frank with her too, and we can laugh over our honesty. She doesn't judge on first appearances.

Bea, 14

That's not to say that there aren't times when even the best of friends won't be irritating to be around. We all get on each other's nerves occasionally. But when you can accept those flaws and love someone anyway, you know the friendship is a keeper.

SOME BEST FRIENDVENTURES

Here are some of my favourite things to do with your friends.

Picnic in the rain
Big boots, even bigger coats and umbrellas galore. Take a flask of tea and a rucksack full of yummy things, plus something to sit on (tarpaulin, plastic sheet – even a shopping bag will do), and enjoy jumping in every puddle you come across and pretending you're five again.

Host a midnight dinner
Illuminate your surroundings with lamps or candles in lanterns, and instruct everyone to arrive in their finest outfits. The more velvet, the better.

Plan a stately visit
Time and money permitting, choose a place you've never been before – whether it's a nearby stately home or a new town you can get to on the train. Turn up and see where the day takes you.

Go wild swimming
Swimming in chilly water is a real thrill, complete with its own inbuilt adrenaline hit. Find an official group to join together so you can swim in

safety. (This is one time you should NEVER jump into the unknown.)

- **Join a campaign**
  What do you care about? Whether it's joining a pre-existing protest group, starting a society in your school, going on a march, or you know, just sitting down with coffee with the specific aim to change the world – get engaged and involved.
- **Have a making day**
  Whether it's art, collages, disastrous scientific experiments, writing poems, making wedding dresses out of newspaper, cake decorating, building a website or starting your own vlogging channel, you are sure to have a good time doing something productive together.

HOW TO BE A GOOD FRIEND

There are tons of lists floating around the internet on this very topic. I'm automatically suspicious of anything that's a 'how to' that doesn't refer to practical stuff like making sure you don't electrocute yourself while retrieving stuck toast from a toaster. How to be a good friend will vary from individual to individual, but here are some possible pointers – not rules – that help to keep any kind of friendship on track.

1) Know when to sit up and listen

An obvious starting place: occasionally we really need someone else's open ear and non-judgemental attitude. There are times to only utter supportive statements.

2) Don't take your friends for granted

No matter how long you have known someone: ask questions. Be curious. Care about what they're up to.

3) Give their romance a chance

Sometimes your friend will have a significant other. If their love interest is ace and you get on brilliantly, you may find having them around is no problem at all. However, this may be tougher if it means your friend stops responding to your texts and cancels on plans – or equally if they give you way too many extended descriptions of exactly what they have been getting up to.

There are several possible avenues for response. One is to accept that at some point, you will also fall madly in love with someone and want to regale your friends with the details of your every encounter. Another is to keep certain topics (i.e. their tongue and your friend's mouth) under a limit in conversation (you may have to simply be blunt and ask them to give you a break from the details, but mind their hurt feelings).

If you don't like this significant other, it's probably best to keep your feelings under wraps – your friend will probably figure out their new boyfriend/girlfriend is not that great a person in time. But there's a big difference between a personality you find grating, and a grade-A arsehole who shouldn't be allowed to date any member of the human race: if you think your friend is being harmed either emotionally or physically, always be a good friend and talk about it, and tell an adult about it too.

4) Take care

Keep an eye out on how your friends are doing. It's very simple, but it means a lot to me when someone notices I'm less sparky than usual, or appear a bit out of sorts. It shows they care enough to register that I'm not quite fine.

5) Be a good cheerleader ...

Be ready to celebrate your friends' successes. Being happy for others is win-win. They feel good, you feel good, they're more likely to celebrate your successes when they come and you can all float together on a fluffy cloud of mutual goodness and happiness.

6) ... But also know that it's human to be jealous

If your friend has got the hairstyle/grades/opportunity you'd kill for – it's ok to feel a little envious. What isn't ok is being bitter or snappy about it. That may be a natural response, but it's also a bad one to let out of its cage. Use your envy productively instead. Spend an afternoon sobbing about why it's not fair, then, identify where your own strengths are and nurture them instead. Get that haircut, put more into your homework, start a blog, begin your plans for being prime minister ... Whatever it is that you're keen to achieve, start working hard towards it – and the best of friends will totally support you in that.

7) Don't be a bitch

Don't talk about your friend behind their back. Make a concerted effort to avoid nastiness. Nothing good ever comes of it, however tempting it may feel to 'let off steam' or 'just be truthful' (or whatever other phrase you want to use to justify what is essentially snark). There was waaaaaay too much bitching in my circle at secondary school, and it was corrosive.

8) Own up if you slip up

Accept that if you do something wrong, and it comes back to bite you, you must own it and apologise. Don't screech 'I didn't, it wasn't me, how could you think that?!?!' Many of us have been found out saying or doing something we shouldn't have. I remember one distinct time where I complained about someone behind their back, and then felt disgustingly guilty when it filtered back to them and they confronted me about it. I said a MASSIVE sorry. It's better to avoid behaving badly, but if you do: make it right!

9) Do nice things (but don't keep a tally)

The best friendships are the ones where you both leave each other buzzing and fizzing with good company. You can only add to that by taking pleasure in doing the odd nice turn: cook your friend a meal, hand-make them a card (glitter galore), concoct a gift, bake a cake … Whatever works, and whatever you know they'll love. Do it for the fun of doing and giving though, rather than keeping count to expect exactly the same amount in return.

PLAYGROUND POWER GAMES

Not every friendship is brilliant. Alongside the magical ones, there are some that exist in name only. Perhaps trust has done a bunk or the constant reordering of *most to least popular* in the group leaves everyone feeling miserable. Although such cliques may dwindle and lose their power in time, that doesn't stop them being hard on you in the meantime (and man, can those times be mean).

I've been there. Oh yes. Been there to the point that I'd wake up dreading school, begging my mum not to make me go. What was the matter? Was I being beaten up? Was I a social outcast? No, nothing as dramatic as that. Instead I was facing a very recognisable scenario – being part of a group of friends, whose behaviour, at times, verged on the very spiteful.

It wasn't consciously malicious, I don't think, but rather a familiar dynamic often found at school – the push and shove of how each girl can assert their social rank. My friend Helen, 19, recalls a similar experience, being part of a big group where they were *'always competitive, undercutting each other'*. That atmosphere of backstabbing and bitching is hard to navigate. Who's at the top? Who's excluding who? Who's secretly talking about the others behind their backs? Who can be laughed at so that everyone else feels closer?

Friendships like these run back to early childhood, where the playground becomes a place of status – where no one wants to be the last one picked for the team and where loyalties are hard to win but easy to lose. High school is an extension of that, with even higher stakes – not to mention more sarcasm and gossip about sex. And, like what you find in the playground, it's a game – a power game. Some people quite simply (and perhaps unconsciously) enjoy having power over others. The ability to make another person feel inadequate can be heady – particularly if it makes up for little power or control elsewhere in life.

In my case, part of the issue was my inability to take part in these games. I've never been great at stepping into a role or sticking to the 'rules' of social setups. I'd often let my vulnerability show, meaning I was an easy target. Girls are quick to pick up on sensitivities and silent awkwardness.

So many small details stabbed deep: Being laughed *at* rather than laughed *with*. Hearing these girls I considered friends join in when outsiders were teasing me. *Knowing* I was being wound up on purpose but remaining unable to keep calm or, occasionally, to hold back my tears. Being left out of conversations or having my request to be told what they were talking about met with blank refusal. Girls 'accidentally' letting slip that so-and-so had said something cruel. The hush of walking into a room and realising that either the group had been talking about me or simply didn't want me there. These events sound insignificant when taken one at a time, but they hurt as they mounted up. The continual feeling was that I was wrong, uncool, undeserving of respect.

There were hundreds of tiny incidents, which built up, at the time. These girls couldn't understand why I hated breaking rules, and would try to drag me in the opposite direction to our classroom when the bell went, laughing at my fear of being late. If one of them wanted to go to the loo, they'd expect a little posse to accompany them there and back – but I had to go by myself. They'd nick things like shoes or homework planners, threatening to throw them on the roof, then giggling as I grew more distressed. On one occasion, when I had thought I couldn't make a birthday sleepover, I realised I had the wrong date. When I excitedly told them I could come after all, I was met with the retort, 'Oh, can't you change the date so you're not here, please?' Many of the good times for them created bad memories for me.

I feel petty itemising these events. But that's the point. They *are* petty – the kind of actions that, now, I just want to roll my eyes at, and shout at all the participants to grow up (while asking my former self to take a stand and tell them where to stick their silly games). But that pettiness almost makes it harder to deal with. You end up wondering if you're justified in feeling upset, and it's easier for others to write the events off as merely a mix of hormones, overreaction and immaturity that'll pass soon enough. Bollocks. It does pass, but it matters too. Dismissing hurt as oversensitivity doesn't help. It's the adult (or teacher) equivalent of the teen response 'God, can't you just take a joke!'

I went through all of that knowing it was not quite wrong, but not quite right either. There were other times that were more challenging to brush off. Once all of them chased me, held me down, and emptied their water bottles over me. This sounds so trivial now, but at the time it was a shock that my friends could behave that way to me.

I know that, when you're being neglected by your friends, it is really tough. Sometimes it's the absolute worst. But I can guarantee that, with time, you'll move on and find much better friends. As you grow and your social circle unfurls further, there'll be ever-more opportunities for meeting people who appreciate you just as you are. Keep hold of that.

> *One of my friends stole from me, lied to me, criticised me, made me feel so small – but apparently it wasn't bullying because we were 'best friends'. My parents told me to just ignore it, thinking it was 'girl problems'.*
> *Emma, 18*

I'm also not saying I was entirely innocent. I got involved in nastiness when others weren't there, and regret some of the snide things I said. It was hard not to join in when we were all involved in this dizzying whirl of sniping and moaning about anyone who left the room. All of us, to varying degrees, were tangled up in this web of bitching and being bitched about. Most of us were just desperate to be accepted – to feel wanted.

You know what? There are plenty of worse things out there than being the only one who doesn't get hugged when people are saying goodbye. But it isn't that single instance. It's the building up of one thing after another until you feel excluded from the group of people you're meant to be friends with.

In between the awful bits, there were sparks of real friendship too. Lovely, close moments of conversation or days spent being really silly. Proper companionship where we laughed so hard our ribs hurt. There were letters written to me, thoughtful presents, genuine compliments, huge heart-to-hearts. We dressed up, watched movies and spent time being artsy. Often these were one-to-one sessions, our relationships were easier if there wasn't an audience to play up to.

It's important to remember the nice parts, for several reasons. First – people change according to who's around them. Someone who's lovely on their own can be horribly different in a group. There's nothing to prove when it's just the two of you, but it's incredibly confusing and upsetting to see someone you've just had an in-depth chat with ignoring you in front of others.

Second – there are always grey areas. Few people are purely mean or entirely angelic. Instead it's a sliding scale. Some people find themselves on the receiving end of a smattering of weird mind games in what is otherwise a pretty great friendship. Others are landed with a shit-storm of malevolence. It is difficult not to see the dark end of that scale as bullying behaviour rather than any kind of friendship, but it can be harder to pick out the differences between good and bad behaviour further up the chart.

Third – the days where these girls were a joy to be around were the reason I stuck with them. All those glimpses showed me what they were capable of, and I craved more. If it had been relentlessly grim, then maybe I'd have found it easier to leave and seek out other people. But these small, marvellous flashes of friendship always made me wonder if it wasn't so bad after all.

Throughout those difficult years, I was so fortunate to have parents I could talk to, and friends who lived elsewhere to rely on – as well as several people outside the group that I *did* get on with at school. My mum was particularly wonderful, spending car journeys and our bedtime chats unravelling everything. We talked about motive, and what drove that kind of behaviour.

From talking it out with my mum, I realised that behind my group's cutting words might lie anything from huge insecurities to a tough family situation. And those problems are worth empathising with. Doesn't mean you necessarily have to accept, forgive, or feel sorry for other people – but it helps to know there's probably a reason behind the odd behaviour and mean, defensive remarks that has absolutely nothing to do with you.

Eventually I found my catalyst for change – spinal surgery. I was off for nearly the entire autumn term in Year Eleven, not properly going back to class until January. Having two metal rods stuck in my back worked wonders ... Spending two months away from the lunchtime politics and petty tricks – well, it was useful. I had plenty of time to think, and re-evaluate my life choices.

Something clicked – mainly a refreshed desire to stop being afraid, and choose carefully how, and with whom, I spent the rest of my time. So I moved on – quite literally. In the first morning registration of the year I waved hello to the old crowd, smiled, then strode across to the other side of the classroom to sit with new people. Some of the girls I spent the rest of that year with remain close friends.

The main thing to bear in mind with friends is this: You're lumped with family. You choose friends. So why go for anyone whose company doesn't leave you feeling buoyant and bubbly and better about the world? If I learned anything from my bad experiences of 'friends' it is that loyalty, mutual appreciation, trust and enthusiasm will make you feel good about yourself. Cattiness, mean comments and manipulation are deflating. Seek out people who appreciate you, who obviously enjoy your company, who 'get' you. Some of us take longer to find these people – but if they're not around right now, I can promise they will be in the future. You might have to work a little harder at finding them, but they're out there. Don't settle for anything less.

Louise O'Neill: The Author

Louise is the award-winning author of *Only Ever Yours* and *Asking For It*. Whether tackling beauty standards or rape culture, her books ask hard questions and point out toxic assumptions about society.

You make great observations about friendships and social status in your books. What was your time like at secondary school? Did that inform what you've written about since?

My time at secondary school was a bit … tempestuous. I fell out with my group of friends when I was about 16 and spent the last couple of years trying to be 'perfect' so that no one would reject me. The strain of attempting to maintain a perfectly pleasant veneer took its toll on me, and my bulimia became rampant. I felt awkward – like I didn't fit in. I think those feelings do inform my writing. I also went to an all girls' school and my experience of a single-sex dynamic is something that has appeared and reappeared in my work.

Both *Only Ever Yours* and *Asking For It* address topics that others tend to shy away from. Do you think, in general, we feel uncomfortable talking about the kinds of things that directly affect young women? And is that changing?

I think that many people dismiss subjects that directly affect girls' lives and trivialise them. Time and time again we have seen that women are silenced, we are told that our stories are not worthy of being told, and this is exasperating when it comes to young women when their age and relative inexperience is used against them. I hope this is changing. Since writing my novels, I have had the privilege of meeting young women frequently and I have found them to be engaging, passionate, and great fun to be around.

Let's talk about selfies. You've written in the past about how they can make you feel either better or worse about your appearance (and yourself in general). I'm pretty keen on a good selfie, and I know you are too. How do you feel about them now?

Like most things in life, I don't think there are any easy answers. I worry when I see young women posting countless selfies a day as I wonder about the value of outsourcing our self-esteem in this way. It can be too easy to depend on how many likes we get. However, I think in a world that tries to encourage women to feel insecure in order to sell them beauty products and clothes, a good selfie can also be an act of defiance. 'Here,' a selfie can say, 'I think I look beautiful today no matter what you say.'

What's been the best thing to come out of writing your books?

Writing both my novels was a deeply cathartic experience. I think I used them to process experiences that had been gnawing at me. I felt much more free after I finished both of them.

MIND THE GAP

It's kind of in-your-face-obvious territory to state that adolescence is a time of change. We tend to mark those changes out in pretty rigid ways, talking about rites of passage like first kisses, new friends, drunken mishaps, parties, sexual experimentation, and all those milestones and etceteras.

Our teens are turbulent for good reason. There's everything to navigate from new schools to a sudden, burning passion for something (or someone) new. Big life changes can happen in an instant or be intense, lengthy episodes. Sometimes they're embedded into the very core of who you are, or perhaps will form the core of who you're developing into. On the other hand, sometimes the physical, mental or emotional changes you experience may be easier for other people to see than they are to you. What may seem like a big event to you might be shrugged off by your friends, and vice versa. Sometimes the changes you go through are wonderful and life-enhancing – at other times they're really bloody hard.

When big changes happen to someone you're close to instead, it's a slightly different ball game. How should you react if your friend suddenly becomes vegan; declares they aren't going to university with you anymore, but are going travelling instead; or just starts getting more and more absorbed with another group of friends? What if one of your friends comes out as gay (which is not necessarily a change – but rather them letting you know something super-crucial about who they are, and always have been) or goes through a whole load of changes after her parents split up?

Changes your friends might go through as you are growing up include *anything*, potentially, and the experience can be confusing or brilliant or terrifying or all of these things and more, depending on the situation. Whatever your friend is facing though, you're well placed to provide some rock-solid support – support that can make all the difference.

Let's take a specific example – gender identity. Definitions of girl and boy are generally spoken about as if each of us neatly slots into one of two options at birth. The expectation is that we will live our lives according to the body we were born into and sure, many of us do. But sex (what's between your legs) and gender (what's between your ears) aren't one and the same. Some people feel a mismatch or divide between the two, or know that neither label is right for them. Rowan, 19, told me, *'I've always had a deep sense of disconnect with the label "man" and unfortunately I was the only girl in an all-boys grammar school.'* Rowan also pointed out that although cultural ignorance is still real and challenging, her friends have been fantastic about her being open about her gender.

It's exasperating that those around you could be anything BUT fabulous and accepting about something as fundamental as being open about your gender identity. Sadly though, as Ruby, who is 14 and transgender relayed to me, comments and insults are still stupidly common.

So how can you help your friend when they go through a big life event? The dictionary meaning of the word 'support' is about bearing the weight of something. Whether we're talking personal problems, family problems or any other tough times, the weights other people bear are their own. You can help to keep your friend going or make the weight more manageable, but those weights are never yours to hold up instead.

Not being able to carry the weight of someone else's problem means two things. 1) You can never really know what someone else is going through, so you have to listen and avoid making assumptions; 2) you have to remember to watch out for yourself too. When my friend was ill with depression I tried to take on responsibilities that weren't mine, and it wasn't healthy for me – or the person I was trying to help. I realised that I needed to be a good friend in the best ways I could BUT (and this is crucial) only while looking after myself too. You're no good to anyone else if you're too drained to function.

HOW TO BE AN AWARD-WINNING FRIEND IN A SUPPORTING ROLE 〰️➡️

I hate to disappoint, but the simple fact is there's no set of rules that somehow guarantee you'll be able to empathise perfectly with what your mates are going through: every one and every situation is different. But there are some fundamentals you can get right:

❋ Listen without making assumptions

It may sound like tired advice, but this simple idea can never be underestimated. In fact we are so used to being told to do it, it's worth stopping and thinking about whether you actually *are* listening.

❋ Don't jump the gun

Try not to say, 'I understand what you're going through' if you don't. And, although it may seem natural to try and link a friend's situation to what seems like more familiar ground – 'Oh, you're going through a break-up. Let me tell you all about when my cat died, and how hard I found that' – best keep those stories to yourself and try and focus on *their* feelings instead. Each person's stories and situations are theirs alone. Learn from them. Let them enlighten you. Your friends will know what they're feeling and thinking much better than you can ever guess.

❋ Do your own research ...

When I was still finding it a bit challenging to get my head around how my best friend's depression meant she could seem totally fine one day, and find the simplest activities impossible the next, she sent me an article all about 'spoon theory'. Look it up (clue, it's not really about cutlery). It's a simple concept that is genuinely brilliant at expressing what it's like living with any kind of illness that drains your energy. If your friend is talking about something that was previously unknown to you, a Google search can yield up a lot of gems. Only good, in general, can come from educating yourself about experiences beyond your own.

🕱 ... But keep your research to yourself

There is a massive difference between looking to find out more about what your friend is going through and then actually telling them what they are going through or worse: what (you think) they should be doing. Your friend knows more about what is happening to them than a million Google searches.

🕱 Do not judge

You may need to unlearn some of the basic misconceptions you've been fed over the years. Golden rule really: enough said.

🕱 Make your support ripple outwards

The other side to all that listening, learning and unlearning? Using your voice. Publicly support and speak up for (without speaking over) your friends. If you hear someone making comments that are judgemental or just plain ignorant? Call it out, calmly, if it feels appropriate (and safe to do so); or at the very least make your feelings known to your friend once the danger has passed. Just because prejudice isn't being levelled directly at you, doesn't mean it's not your problem. In fact, you're in a good position to challenge it – rather than remaining a bystander.

Beyond all these things, the best way you can offer your friend support is by giving them that most precious of things – time. Time to grow and alter and dive into the unfamiliar and explain what's going on. Time – and patience – for their occasional mood swings and bad behaviour during the tricky bits; and don't forget to share some joy in the great moments. Sometimes the nicest thing you can do when they're having a horrible week is something thoughtful. If my friends are struggling, I try and clear an evening so that I can cook them dinner, or drag them to watch a movie. Simple things, but that's sometimes what you need when life's a bit all over the place – a dose of the mundane and the familiar. Of course, it could be a chance to suggest you have an outrageous dressing-up session too. Depends on what feels right.

It can be in the small details too: postcards, unexpected goody bags, or a text about something stupid and embarrassing you've done and wanted to share with your usual partner in crime. It shows that you're there, you care, you've noticed they need a boost, and you give a damn about their wellbeing.

None of these necessarily *solve* anything – but that's because being a good friend is not about solving. You don't have to do that – and you probably can't solve most of the problems your friends will knock up against. All you can do is be there when necessary. Give room for laughter if needed, or let them cry. What's important is that regardless of what is going on, the stupid in-jokes and small gestures and wonderful conversations and the simple pleasure of hanging out won't disappear. These funny little things that make a friendship may alter for a while, but that's ok. True friendships are about weathering unexpected circumstances, as well as having fun.

ME, MYSELF AND I

Whether you are talking about friendships or any other kind of relationship, the one you have with yourself is key. What's the secret formula to unlocking this? Well, the truth is, spending time by yourself is fantastic. It took a while for me to realise how liberating being on your own can be. Not everything has to be done with someone else in tow. Alone doesn't equate to lonely. Being on your own doesn't have to mean being a social outcast. That may be the view promoted by high school movies, where loyalty to a friendship group is everything and only quirky and/or sad outsiders sit by themselves, but it's crap.

Instead, a little self-indulgence, and self-care, is truly wonderful. You don't have to splash out on an expensive day at the shops. 'Me-time' isn't only about spending money on yourself (although that can obviously be nice). Instead it's the power of knowing when to prioritise yourself.

Some people might call that selfishness. I disagree. It's important to look beyond your own life and be there for others too – but it's nigh on impossible to support anyone else if you're not supporting yourself. Being go-go-go all the time can be fab (and useful for those who thrive on structure and being busy), but knowing when to stop is just as key.

For me, this usually means letting go of fears over missing out – of feeling that if I don't go to a particular party or festival then I'm not living life as fully as I should. It doesn't really matter if you bail on a particular event. There are always others. Sometimes it's good to challenge yourself to say 'no' and stay in, or spend some time in your own company in the same way that it's healthy for introverts to say 'yes' to a scary-sounding night out.

I often find I'm more productive and sociable too when I do the stuff I really enjoy that doesn't make me stressy and exhausted. Having a lie-in. Spending a whole day cooking for my friends. Poking around a few boutiques I can't afford to shop in. It allows me to slow down, re-calibrate, take measure of what's going on. It's refreshing. Besides, most of us love being treated well by others – so why not begin with being good to yourself first?

UNDER PEER PRESSURE

Sex and drugs and social roles are all 'Issues' with a capital 'I' often associated with peer pressure, and are the subject of countless work sheets, school assemblies and Teen Guides.

At some point in your teen years, you're let free from parental supervision and get to experiment and push boundaries. Suddenly you're formulating your own tastes – what you enjoy, what you don't. There's more independence, but also more pressure to do the same things as everyone else.

Conformity is a funny thing. In many ways, I think it's a better term than peer pressure – mainly because it digs a little deeper.

You might not think that your desire to wear certain clothes or hang out with a particular group is the result of those around literally 'pressuring' you into doing so – but there's more than likely an element of wanting to fit in, or to find a community.

The pressure to fit in with a group goes on in adulthood too, but there's something unique to teenagers: school. It's a bubble, a place with its own unspoken codes and types of conduct, with hierarchies assembled over time. The domain of classroom and corridors heightens everything – hard to escape when you spend so much of your week there.

The funny thing is that each school will have its own measure of what's desirable and what's not. At my school being cool was all about bitching about other people. But I also have friends who attended schools full of raging competition to be the best at everything academic.

Is there any quick solution to avoid or defeat peer pressure? No, not really. I guess you could stop caring about acceptance, or let go of the frustration at what gets celebrated as 'cool', or just decide to full stop not give a f***.

But deciding is only half the battle. Acting on it is harder. And sometimes it just feels safer to keep your head down, and get through it until you can finally move on. Well whatever works. Just remember: peer pressure can be a bit of a monster. Recognise it when it rears its ugly head.

HAPPY HOUR?

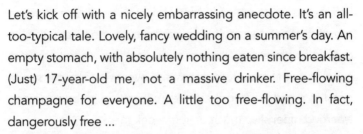

Let's kick off with a nicely embarrassing anecdote. It's an all-too-typical tale. Lovely, fancy wedding on a summer's day. An empty stomach, with absolutely nothing eaten since breakfast. (Just) 17-year-old me, not a massive drinker. Free-flowing champagne for everyone. A little too free-flowing. In fact, dangerously free ...

My memories get more fogged as the evening goes on. I can just about picture the awful dancing, my still-brimming glass sloshing around in one raised hand. Thankfully I can't recall the journey across London afterwards. There are fragments. Me trying to put on what I thought were my flat shoes, but that actually belonged to the four-year-old bridesmaid. Being frog-marched to the train, one parent gripping each shoulder, and still tumbling over. Being washed in the bath when we finally got back. Conveniently, for my own sake, the part I have no memory of whatsoever is throwing up everywhere – on the train, down my dress, in my handbag. It wasn't attractive, to say the least.

There were consequences. The first was a gut-curdling sense of shame (and a killer hangover). My parents didn't need to tell me off. They could see I was already angry with myself. I apologised again and again and again. I knew my dad had done much worse in his youth, but I felt awful. Awful that I'd been a mess, awful that my parents were terrified they wouldn't manage to get me back to where we were staying because I was so far gone, awful that my brother had seen me behave this way and was scared by it.

Our culture often celebrates excess – getting wasted, hammered, trashed, past control. I have no desire to reach any of those states again. Maybe there's some bizarre thrill in getting so drunk that you can't use your legs and needing to expel the contents of your stomach everywhere, but if so, it's one I'm happy to forgo. I've been drunk since, but never to that kind of level.

Most people have got a similar story to mine – some much more gruesome, and usually at a younger age (living in the countryside, plenty of my peers shared the rural rite of passage of spewing up cider in a field in the middle of nowhere). But I didn't really drink before sixth form, and barely went clubbing until I got to uni. I have a handful of friends whose teenage years hardly resemble mine: stories that were hair-raising, to put it mildly.

Abbie, now 23, took a lot of drugs in her teens, but said to me *'I wouldn't do that now, but because it isn't sensible. I didn't even consider the fact that I could die, that I could get really ill – it was just about fun. Being a teenager you don't have any sense of consequences.'*

WHY ARE DRUGS SO DANGEROUS? 〰➤

It's partly the feeling of invincibility – the lack of awareness of your own vulnerability – that can be harmful. For example, drugs affect people in a variety of ways. Some drugs don't seem to have much of a side effect, apart from the people taking them becoming more boring and self-involved as the night goes on. Others can make you suffer really seriously: some can kill you instantly. People who take drugs might accidentally overdose, or take something that isn't what it looks like, or get into trouble because they are behaving dangerously, or finish the night in the back of an ambulance, or end up triggering an underlying health condition. Drug taking is always risky, as you never know the quantity or quality of what you're taking. Since these substances are illegal, there is no quality control: they could literally be *anything*. I find that terrifying. Drugs are not legal, and the ways they are grown, manufactured, and transported are not monitored, and can be more deadly and disgusting than you can imagine.

We have this notion that the most exciting way to be is out of control and spontaneous – the life and soul of the party, the thrill-seeker. But the stereotypical teen image isn't an accurate portrait of anyone in particular. Going to a party and dancing all night might be the thrilling highlight of your week, but for other people it can be a cause of anxiety, or exasperation.

In some groups, it's quite common to feel like the odd teen out if you're not spending half your time upsetting your parents with your unknown whereabouts. But actually you're very normal if you have no desire to get drunk, get high or get off with someone else. I think a lot of the time we act in a particular way out of fear of being seen as boring. But who defines 'boring'? Some of the most boring evenings I've had involved watching others get more and more out of control and wishing I was somewhere – anywhere – else.

THE GHOST OF FRIENDSHIPS PAST

I must admit it was odd recalling everything that mattered so much at secondary school – the desire to be liked, the friendship battles, the at times desperate desire to fit in.

Like most things, once you're beyond it, it's simple to reduce down to a few memories, wondering why you couldn't have been braver at the time. Having written it all down, I realised how frustrated I was at having spent that long in an unhappy situation. But it is important to look at your past without reducing it to a few key events, even if it requires more effort to remember how it really felt then. The rules and ways of being accepted that may seem ridiculous from the outside are harder to put into perspective when you're working through them. I was not able to step away from that group of friends – telling my mum 'You don't understand, I can't, I just can't' whenever she asked why I spent my free time with people who left me unhappy. I was afraid that I'd end up completely isolated, forever bereft of friends.

Now I can see how far I've moved beyond those worries, they feel trivial now. At the time they weren't – back then it was horrible – but it's nice to know how much has changed since. Now I spend lots of time happily by myself. I don't bother with friendships where the other person doesn't put in any effort. I'll speak up if someone behaves towards me in a way I don't appreciate. Perhaps those grim early teen years paid off – now I value all my wonderful, warm friendships immensely.

I feel no bitterness towards anyone I hung out with at school. I'm frustrated at how I let it all get to me, yes, but I'm not angry with the individuals themselves. Many of them had their own stuff going on. In any case, we were all trying to work out who we were and how we fit into that small social world.

Secondary school is strange and intense. But people grow up – and more importantly, they grow out of certain behaviours. They change, they evolve, people who hurt you can become close friends (and vice versa). Someone who you share everything with at one point in your life might have nothing in common with you soon after. It's fine to drift apart. Better to commit to relationships that are still alive and kicking, rather than those that have slowly stopped mattering.

I don't see why it should always be nasty when people stop being friends. Sometimes you just reach a point where you don't fit together anymore. That's natural, and it makes room for the people you do fit with.

Poppy, 19

Between the friends you already have and the potential to expand your social life – more people, more conversations, more experiences – there's a lot of fun to be had. And who better to share it with than your extraordinary, brilliant mates?

AAARGH!? LOVE!

For years I was convinced that no one would ever find me attractive, let alone want to be in a relationship with me. While other girls seemed to manage just fine, flirting their way through lunchtime, getting off with the guys they liked at parties and later declaring that they'd lost their virginity, I felt like the odd one out.

Obviously, there were just as many of us *not* summoning a small crowd to give whispered details of exactly *what* had happened on the weekend – but we weren't as vocal. It seemed like kissing and hugs and spooning and sex were the only things worth being talked about – the activities that gave short-term status and membership to the gang claiming to be in the know.

Looking back, I can see my behaviour was coloured by an understandable mix of disdain and nervousness. I had the occasional crush, but these dwindled by the end of Year Eight when I realised that liking someone on looks alone had a pretty big downside.

It got harder to ignore being relentlessly single when I began sixth form. People matured, and were much less likely to bunch up in a circle shouting 'fight, fight, fight' while watching two Year Nines get progressively muddier as they grappled. But I remained, to use a phrase I put in my diary in a bizarrely Jane Austen-esque tone, 'to my displeasure, horribly single'.

I ended up with a weird double-anxiety. I knew that I just hadn't found anyone where it mutually clicked, and didn't want to invest in anything I wasn't interested in. But still, but still ... Why did my friends get asked out, and I got ignored? How did they manage to go from relationship to relationship? Was I doing something wrong? Was I not attractive, not interesting, not good enough? Was I just shit at flirting? (Answer to the last one at least is easy – yes, yes I was.)

These kinds of questions may feel melodramatic, but then again, it's very easy to wind yourself up until it feels like you're the only person in the whole universe who has never been asked out.

We live in a society where it's assumed that you'll have had at least one major relationship by your 20s, that it's strange if you're yet to experience proper 'first love' by the end of your teens. But there's no such thing as a standard trajectory, or sell-by date on when things should be done. Although my first kiss was your typical hmm-this-isn't-quite-what-I-imagined-and-ooh-there's-a-tongue, it happened much later than all of my friends. Now I have a litany of funny tales and encounters I occasionally take great pleasure in relaying to my friends. But secondary school me just couldn't see that ever being the case. She hoped that one day someone amazing might magically appear, but the gap between reality and this ideal future seemed impossible to bridge.

My experience, although not uncommon, still felt like it stuck out when compared to my friends. There are many other people who had teenage relationships that were super-significant. Of course. Flirting and falling for people and being part of a couple is wonderful, and sometimes demanding, but always formative: you learn something about yourself and other people every step of the way. It just takes some of us longer than others to get there.

Plus, it's not just those that you actively end up 'in' a relationship with either. There are so many other learning curves and detours: remember the usually gross but somehow still exciting rounds of truth or dare, the on-the-spot kisses you weren't anticipating, the bloody awful limpet-like snogs, the people you're not really sure about, the people you were sure about who turn out to be slimy, the hurt when the object of your affections is oblivious to your existence, the friends you try kissing but it just feels weird, the friends you like but it's never acknowledged, the giddy feelings of 'what if' and 'just maybe' (as well as the slump of 'oh dear, maybe not').

Then there's the jelly-legged joy of glimpsing whoever it is you totally fancy, the thrill when it's intimated that they might just feel the same way. The flirting you didn't mean, the flirting they didn't mean. Hope, disappointment, surprise, suspense. No wonder so many books and films revolve around relationships, both the successful and the disastrous ones.

WHY *DO* WE CARE SO MUCH ABOUT RELATIONSHIPS?

We spend more time worrying about our partners (or the lack of them) than all other types of relationships. We talk about BIG relationships in terms of 'soul mates' or 'the one'. The same kind of language – of closeness, individuality and completion – doesn't get applied to friendships. Katie, 16, pointed out to me that: *'People are seen as needing another person to be truly whole.'*

Why is this? Maybe because romantic companionship is ever so compelling. Most – although not all – of us want to seek out someone special to share our time with. Evie, 17, said to me, *'Most people have had a friendship that's been lovely – but this is more than a friendship, because they're yours, and you are theirs. You guys share something special. The intimacy – the physical, personal element. It's a mutual belonging to each other.'*

Being close to someone else, being vulnerable – without any of the usual social armour – can be exhilarating, but also scary. It requires a level of trust – one that (hopefully) then leads to a sense of being entirely comfortable around one another. It provides support, a structure, plenty of new experiences.

I started going out with my boyfriend at 13. We had our third anniversary the other day. My friends have had loads more experiences, but I think I prefer being with the same person. I'm his first girlfriend, he's my first boyfriend – we have that connection.

Jemima, 16 📢

But other people aren't interested in finding their true love in their school years. Celia, 15, observed *'Boys are just quite annoying at 15 – they're not very mature! Being with some random person for the sake of it isn't worth it – you want to be with someone who you really like.'* I think that's a really important point: Relationships aren't worth going into merely for the sake of being in one. A new relationship should be about the fizz and flutter of reciprocated feeling. And arguments over who forgot to text who back, obviously.

RECIPE FOR A GOOD RELATIONSHIP 〰➤

This recipe comes with a disclaimer. Pick only the best ingredients, and season your choices with care. This recipe has no use-by date.

✱ 1) Take five ounces of flirting and whisk gently with a handful of new opportunities, roughly chopped. Shake in several drops of enthusiasm, and a pinch of openness to the unexpected.

✱ 2) Heat gently over a low flame while stirring in a cup of communication and a big dollop of honesty. This is a key ingredient – one that this recipe can't do without.

✱ 3) Toast a large packet of genuine kindness (found in all good specialist stores) with half a teaspoon of raucous adventures. Scatter over the mixture, which should now be airily light.

Note: Some natural separation may occur now and then, but improves the overall flavour when everything is mixed back together.

WHY BEING BRAVE ISN'T SUCH A BAD THING

You know what's great? Taking a deep breath and doing what scares you. Some things may be scary for good reason. Stuff like walking too close to cliff edges or taking part in sword fights. Don't do those. Impending doom aside, however, there are lots of other actions that might make your heart beat a little faster – but are all the more worth doing as a result.

Stuff like going up to that person who you think looks interesting (or who you already know), and asking if they fancy going for a coffee/to the cinema/hanging out/whatever else you fancy. At the very least, it's guaranteed to be more effective than screaming that you like them, accidentally kicking them in the shins and then running away.

Ok. I must admit that advice is a lot easier to give out than to act on. Plonk me in a big meeting with lots of adults, and I'm fine. Not a jolt of anxiety. Seeing someone I fancy? Different story. Trembling hands aplenty.

But I've still done it. I've given people the eye and introduced myself and taken that first step into the unknown. No, it hasn't always worked. But at least I took the chance. And for every time I've plucked up the courage, there are probably two more where I've kicked myself for not being proactive and instead retreating, suddenly looking aloof and icy because I'm nervous.

On the other hand, the day I stopped berating myself for letting those chances slip away was a very good one. I said to myself: Hang on, this is silly. Why am I being disappointed for not striking up a conversation when they could have very easily begun talking to me too? All the effort doesn't have to come from my end. Oh happy, happy realisation.

Be brave as often as you can. Occasionally do the things that make your stomach flip, but see it as a new opportunity and reward yourself for trying rather than feeling like a failure if it goes a bit pear-shaped. If sometimes you just want to curl up into a little snail shell of shame and shyness, you're as human as human can be. But climb back out of your shell the next day and welcome that oh-so-familiar overwhelming, startling, brilliant, nausea-inducing mix of emotions.

WHEN YOU HAVE TO TURN SOMEONE DOWN

Just as it takes a lot of guts to walk away with your head held high when the object of your affection isn't interested, there is a certain art to saying thanks, but no thanks.

For the main, being asked out is an internal 'YESSSS' moment of relief, the elation of realising that your sly glances and idle daydreams weren't all one-way. Or maybe it's unexpected, but you'll still be intrigued and flattered. Then again, maybe it's someone you get on with incredibly well, though only as friends. Or worse case scenario: maybe it's a stranger who you want to get as far away from as possible because you're getting vibes that screech 'creepy'. With the latter, never feel bad about removing yourself or asking them to leave you alone. You don't owe your time or attention to anyone making you feel uncomfortable.

Let's take the slightly more mundane situation for our example – where you get asked out by someone who you already know, but don't fancy. Is there an effective formula for delivering your rejection with gentleness, especially if you respect and like the person doing the asking?

In times of need, there's a limited bank of stock phrases that we tend to draw on: 'Can we just remain mates?'; 'I'm not looking for a relationship at the moment'; 'Aaargh, umm, well, thanks but, well, errrrm, I don't feel the same'. Millions rely on the same words to tackle these complicated, personal things. How many times has the ear of the universe picked up the phrase 'I really like you, but just as a friend'? Well, don't feel bad if you use one of these phrases in a time of need. It's because they're easy words, well worn with use. Being articulate when you've been put on the spot isn't easy, particularly if the question came totally out of the blue.

So what can you do beyond borrowing a well-known answer? Be honest and sensitive. Not overly honest in a listing-every-reason-it-wouldn't-work way. If you think they're ace, just not romantically, say that – and explain why you enjoy hanging out with them, but nothing more. If you don't know them very well, but recognise that it probably took courage to ask you out, remain gracious – but firm. Obviously none of these are hard and fast rules. Everyone has their own way of tackling these scenarios.

Also don't be afraid to make your boundaries clear, especially if someone oversteps the mark. This advice is also true when someone hasn't made a grand declaration, but their admiration is more transparent than a newly washed window. If you've gently rebuffed someone several times to little effect, don't be afraid of being blunt.

An additional note: if you know someone likes you (either because they've told you as much, or it's obvious) it's easy to play up to it, to indulge in their attraction to you, but keep them at arm's length. Many people are seduced not by the person, but by the attention.

We're taught to value ourselves because of our relationships – the partners we have, the people we attract, the stories we can tell (my general rule is the more disastrous the encounter, the more entertaining the anecdote). And of course, there's a lot of gratification to be had in knowing that someone thinks you are pretty damn awesome.

But something I learnt the very hard way was this – there's a big difference between wanting someone in particular, and just wanting to be wanted. Several times I've fallen into the trap of *thinking* I like someone when actually it's more to do with my own ego. The desire to be desired, the need to be needed, overrides the actual question of attraction.

There's nothing wrong in wanting someone else to find you beautiful or interesting or a pleasure to be around. But there's a difference between that and pursuing someone in the hope that they might just briefly make you feel good about yourself. If all the work is coming from your end, then it's not worth it. These people *won't* validate you by telling you how much they think you're beautiful or interesting or a pleasure to be around. They're not fab enough to see it.

THE GNAWING PAIN OF UNREQUITED LOVE

One of my favourite ever films is *Cinema Paradiso* – an Italian movie charting a boy's relationship with his local cinema. It's gorgeous. All about stories and time and growing up and moving beyond the place that shaped you. There's a particularly interesting sequence where the protagonist,

Salvatore, tries to woo the object of his attractions, Elena, by spending night after night standing outside her house. She steadily ignores him at first. They do, however, eventually get together. In reality, few of us have the willpower to be that committed. And THANK GOD. As lovely as it may look on screen, in reality it's really, really weird.

That long preamble aside, unrequited love hurts. Oh it hurts. It's uniquely crushing when you have very strong feelings towards someone who is either oblivious or not interested (or just totally, utterly out of bounds). The sting is readily dismissed by other people too, which makes the whole thing worse. Georgina, 17, commented on the frustration of this, saying, *'Being in a vulnerable position at 15 or 16, when someone doesn't like you back, really hurts.'* Your parents say 'Oh, teenage love, teenage romance. How painful!' But yes, it *is* painful.

When your feelings towards someone are unrequited, it's frustrating, but also out of your control. Even if you were wittiest, funniest, most brilliant human being ever (without being insufferable too, which would be quite the achievement), try as you like, you still wouldn't be able to change that person's perception of you.

My mum has a great phrase she uses in situations like these: you're knocking at the wrong address. The premise is simple. If you're looking for the right address – in this case, someone who will appreciate you because you're *you* – then there's no point looking for it in places where you're not going to find that. It's oh so easy to seek validation from those who are never going to give it, or to lust after individuals who sadly aren't going to turn round and suddenly sweep you up in a cloud of declarations and kisses. I know. Dammit. But they aren't. Sorry. Not gonna happen. So start looking for the right addresses instead.

If you like someone, and they don't like you back, all you can do is acknowledge that it's the worst – but that it'll pass, eventually. Even if takes a really long time and lots of angry music.

FRIEND ZONE THIS, BUSTER

When it comes to unrequited love stories, it's easy to like the actions of a quirky hero gently wooing the object of his affections. But in reality, *Cinema Paradiso* behaviour would be pretty weird. Hollywood all too often includes a storyline where, when a woman says no, she is just playing hard to get and if the hero wears away at her resolve for long enough (or violently enough), she'll realise that she loves him after all. Bullshit, anyone?

While we are on the subjects of unrequited love and playing hard to get, and leading people on, there are a few misconceptions to clear up: specifically those connected to the friend zone. Sometimes it's an accurate description for the kind of situation where someone you reeeeeeeeeeeaaaaally like deftly slots you into the category of 'friend' with a wink and a smile – so ensuring a very clear lack of any possible romance. It's a sad zone, full of pleasant smiles, rather than fabulous kisses.

But the 'friend zone' has also taken on a weird aspect: a way of suggesting that if the object of someone's affections doesn't return their good-friend behaviour with love (or, to be frank, sex), then there's something unfair going on. I'm talking about the idea that if a guy lets a girl cry on his shoulder and supports her through a tough time, and she doesn't then respond to a sexual advance from him in a positive way, he has been 'put in the friend zone', in the same way you put unruly toddlers 'in time out'.

There are multiple levels of shit here. Firstly, it suggests that being lovely to someone else requires reward, rather than just appreciation. It also implies that (usually) women owe (often) male friends their time or love or their bodies in return for those friends being, well, friends.

This is frustrating all on its own because it suggests that guys and girls can't just be friends (or at least not without a big dose of sexual tension) – which is a crock of crap. It's interesting that it's used almost entirely (though not always) by self-professed 'nice guys' who feel that girls have rejected them.

A girl being friendly is not leading someone on. A girl sharing her vulnerabilities is not leading someone on. A girl treating someone as a confidante or somebody she likes by spending time with them is not leading someone on. However, someone acting the part of a friend just to get into a girl's knickers is not a 'nice guy' and frankly, *is* leading the girl on. He's no kind of friend.

It also twists something genuinely hard – liking someone and them not liking you back – into a question of entitlement. No one is entitled to romance, let alone sex. It feels beyond miserable if you have the hots for someone and it's not reciprocated. If that's the case, you can suck it up or stop seeing them if it's too painful – but letting resentment fester isn't healthy, or fair on anyone.

JUST ME?

When it seems like you're the only one not in on some great experience that all and sundry are talking about, it can feel incredibly isolating – I know, I've been there. Dina, 19, said to me that as a teen she was *'really jealous of friends who were in relationships,'* adding that, *'all teenage TV programmes cover relationships. I think it's unfair to give that to teenagers and say "look, this is what your life is meant to be like and if you're not ticking those boxes, then what's wrong with you?"'*

So many more people are lonely than it looks. Just because others appear happy or blissfully loved up, it doesn't mean they are. That's not lemon-faced cynicism – more an acknowledgment that everyone has a whole hidden, inward world of feelings and anxieties and joys.

At times it may feel like you are alone or unloved when everyone else has got it sorted. But who knows if they really have? Pretending everything's ok – that's easy. Being honest? Harder. We're not encouraged to be open about feelings, so we get good at presenting a front. As a result, sometimes we don't realise how common our worries are – and just how many other people we know are in a similar position.

Even if your friends are happily coupled up at the moment, there is a much bigger world out there: you're not alone if you're feeling alone. It's really ok if you've never been in a relationship – or if you've not been in one for a long time. Hopefully you're content with that, and are enjoying the time, freedom and space to yourself. But if you're feeling a bit miserable at not having found the right person yet? I totally get it. Ugh, it's the worst.

Being independent, confident and secure in yourself are all fantastic ways to be. If no one else is recognising that, as much as I hate to admit it, it's frustrating. Regardless of whether you possess confidence and independence, you're definitely brilliant. But sadly it can take a while to find the right person sometimes. I'm also not going to say that your Mr or Mrs Right is out there, just waiting to be stumbled across. I don't know if they are or not. I'd hope so, but who knows? Some people find him or her easily, others take much longer – as infuriating as that is. My advice? Keep looking, and enjoy some 'me' time!

FIVE WAYS TO TAKE YOURSELF ON A DATE 〰➤

Just like planning a special evening for that superhot guy or girl, there's a fine art to dating yourself.

✱ Take yourself out for a fancy breakfast. Sling a book in your bag, or whatever else you want to keep yourself occupied with, and ask for a table for one. Eat a giant stack of pancakes and watch the world go by.

✱ Borrow a serious-looking thermos and go spend a day in the nearest forest. Great for clearing the head, lifting the heart, and plenty of other clichés. Honestly, going for a long tramp on your lonesome can be magical. It's a time for feet to move and thoughts to unspool.

✱ Surprise yourself with something you've been wanting for ages. A film you forgot to see in the cinema? That lovely bracelet you saw a few weeks ago? An album that's just been released? Gift wrap your memories and marvel at how thoughtful you are to yourself.

✱ Go and sun yourself. Pile on sun cream and pack a little picnic with care. Spread your blanket, laze around and enjoy some strawberries in the sunshine.

✱ Surreptitiously check your diary when you're not looking so that you can find a clear day to propose a trip to the seaside. Take yourself to the beach to poke around the shore or eat ice cream on the pier.

HOLLYWOOD IS NO LOVE DOCTOR

Certain types of Romance with a capital R – think rose petals, rustling silk sheets and ridiculously over-the-top costume-drama style declarations – have fallen far out of fashion. Unsurprising. Our lives are too busy for ball gowns and chaperoned tea parties and mysterious strangers that appear without warning on dark nights. It's simpler without the frippery too.

But love is still talked about constantly – thousands of words are published on it, a national holiday is dedicated to it … Ok, a single day invented by big companies to make lots of money out of cards, chocolates and flowers. Love, we are told, is a many splendour'd thing, something we can't live without. Romantic fiction sells in truckloads, while Hollywood studios are financed by audiences buying into movies about passion and heartbreak. These worlds are safe, contained, easy to escape into.

Sometimes these films do capture the reality – more complex, messier, relationships, at the very least requiring some compromise. They get that mixture of wonder and angst. But the reality of relationships, wonderful as they can be, is often a little more everyday. There's likely to be stewing resentment over lack of communication, as well as the pleasure of knowing how much you mean to someone else.

I'm often struck by the big influence of the narratives we read, watch and listen to though. Most people *do* realise that the Disney happy ending is a myth. We're aware that things aren't sorted with a kiss and a sprinkle of stardust – and that, actually, getting married to someone you barely know just because he happened to turn up, flip his ridiculous hair and try to rescue you from some mildly scary situation isn't romantic, but creepy.

But what about all the plotlines that aren't so in-your-face obvious? The one where, if a girl goes to a café by herself or catches a train, it'll just so happen that a lovely young someone strikes up a conversation with her. The one where, after a series of will-they-won't-they mishaps, friends finally get together and everything is wrapped up neatly, with a little bow on top. All those instances where sex *just happens* – where condoms are never mentioned, foreplay hasn't been invented and nobody farts.

Where's this going, other than a rant about how life isn't like the movies? Well by and large these storylines and characters not only set up unrealistic attitudes, but actually encourage dodgy gender expectations in a really insidious way.

We're not just massive sponges assimilating everything around us until we're merely made up of what we've seen. Rather, it's the very subtle ways these things infiltrate our sense of what *should* happen. We spend a vast proportion of our life consuming media, so it's unsurprising it has an influence. But it's always worth picking apart that influence, asking yourself what effect it has on your identity and how you see the world.

Sometimes your underlying assumptions can get the better of you. Elizabeth, 16, talked to me about her first boyfriend, saying *'For some reason, I became convinced that the only way I would be able to impress him was if we liked all the same things. I became that girl who agreed with everything he said. Even when I disliked an album, or wanted to go somewhere else, I'd nod along because I believed that was what I needed to do. When I was brash and opinionated, boys looked at me like I was a bit weird, but when I nodded along, boys kissed me and said I looked beautiful ... And, oh god, I had that all upside down and back to front and completely messed up.'*

After a while she realised that she could, and should, go her own way instead. She realised it was pretty much pointless to try and shape yourself to fit someone else. She later added that *'I understand now that it's not worth the time and effort to effectively put my own life on hold just to shape myself into someone's sidekick, or girlfriend, or whatever.'*

Like Elizabeth, it took me a little while to reach the point of recognising that compromising your identity or interests never works out – whether you're trying to impress a potential partner or your social group. Write your own script, rather than playing a bit part in someone else's. It's much more fun, and vastly more rewarding.

LET'S ALL TALK MORE ABOUT SEX

As we all know, the legal age of consent in the UK is 16. But awareness of sex and sexuality begins for most way before that age. Between playground chatter, TV and movies, music and books and the pervasive presence of online porn, anyone who reaches their 16th birthday without having discussed or thought about sex must been living under a particularly isolated rock.

Yet here lies a problem: although the conversation may have started, I'm certainly not recommending anyone under 16 jumps the gun. The law's there for good reason. It's in place to keep people safe, acknowledging that a hell of a lot of maturing happens in those crucial teen months and years. Where the alteration to a person between age 24 and 26 may seem negligible, there's a huge difference between 14 and 16. You're growing, learning, maturing and taking things on board all the time.

Somewhere in between all of that, people begin talking about sex – and talking A LOT. By about Year Nine, it seems to become *the* hot topic, whether it's boasting in the playground, late night chats with friends, or a hurricane of whispers about what two people got up to behind the bins last Wednesday (which, I might add, probably didn't actually take place). And oh my god, it can seem so terrifying, especially when others already appear ridiculously confident and in-the-know (clue: they're probably not).

To come back to that phrase, the 'age of consent', there's an important word here – *consent*. Probably *the* most important word when it comes to sex, in all sorts of ways. It covers everything from communication to power to emotional readiness to decision making. Yet it's a word many still aren't clear about the meaning of. So why is it crucial? Actually, those four areas I just mentioned are a good starting point …

Communication

Consent is all about talking, asking, listening and responding. It's about making boundaries clear, discussing what you're comfortable with, and being frank about staying safe. It's also about getting a keen 'Yes!' from both sides to any activity. The smallest sign of a 'no' and it's literally 'no-go'. It's about the non-verbal stuff too. It's easy to tell the difference between enthusiasm and unease or discomfort. Nervousness is ok. Body language suggesting 'I don't want to do this' (or any phrase like 'I'm not sure/maybe not now/I'm really tired' as well as outright silence) is not ok, and should be noticed, respected and responded to by backing off. Anyone who doesn't do that is not a good person to be with. Oh and on the subject of staying safe, as Abbie, 23, said to me, *'I've always had no problem saying, "right, where's the condom?" You just can't be too embarrassed for that.'*

Power

For starters, anyone in a position of status – a teacher, official figure, group leader or instructor – is completely off limits, as you can't give someone who is already in a position of power your consent: the relationship is already skewed. Once someone is in a role of trust, they should never do something that would take advantage of that position.

Other people can upset the power balance too. Any time someone is pressuring you into things you don't want to do, that's just not right. At all. You don't owe anyone anything. No one else should manipulate or guilt-trip you into anything, or do something completely dickish like suggest that you're lucky they find you attractive. Doesn't matter if you're in a relationship with that person. Not even if you've done stuff together before. Nuh-uh. This is something to go into equally, on your own terms, every time – not with someone else telling you what to do.

If you think someone is pressuring someone you know into sex, be a good friend about it: offer your support, listen to their story, and always make sure an adult knows what is going on.

A last word about power: sex is supposed to be *fun*. Any talk that a guy is supposed to enjoy it more than a woman is just wrong. Don't let anyone tell you otherwise.

Emotional readiness
Part of emotional readiness – which means being able to deal with all the weird whooshy hormones and mood swings that come with big physical relationships – is the whole being 16 years old or over thing, obviously. But it goes deeper than reaching that number of years: The 'being emotionally ready

for this' bit is pretty damn crucial. Only you can know this. No one else can. There are no hard and fast rules about readiness: You might be just about ready by the time you're 16, or it may take a few years beyond that. It takes some of us longer than others, and for a world of different reasons. Part of it is about taking care of yourself too – just in knowing that your body is pretty great, and you deserve for it to only be appreciated by people who will treat it well. It shouldn't feel rushed.

Decision making

Be smart, and safe, about any kind of sex. Discuss contraception AND protection (for same-gender relationships as well, and for 'not going all the way' sexy stuff too). Make sure any thing you do is something you're actively choosing to do because you want to, rather than passively accepting because it feels like you should or it's what the other person is pushing for. The only person who can ever decide that you want to have sex is, well, *you*. Your life. Your body. Your decisions.

IS IT REALLY THAT EMBARRASSING TO TALK ABOUT SEX?

So, care to talk about sex? I think that's exactly what we should all do more of – have honest, direct, non-judgemental discussions about it much more often. This should include talking about sex as a physical activity with consequences – and as an emotional event that can affect your mind and the way you feel and behave. More importantly, we shouldn't just talk about how to be sensible and safe, but how to enjoy it, in a frank and open way.

Teens can grow up feeling ashamed about sex, because from a young age, we get the sense we shouldn't talk about it. But I think if you're ashamed, then you're less likely to make positive choices. And it's crucial to be talking about all sides of sex *before* you're at a point where you're considering doing it. That way there's readily available information, an understanding of what is ok and what is NOT ok, clear knowledge about not getting pregnant or contracting STIs, and having a healthy, balanced attitude. With all the focus on the ugly side of sex, is anyone telling us about how to enjoy it? Erm, surely that's pretty important too.

At the moment, the main source of info for teens is school-delivered sex ed. The domain of condoms on plastic penises and terrifying pictures of STIs. Is this really going to prepare us for healthy adult relationships? Most lessons present sex as purely physical behaviour, with generally pretty nasty consequences. Sex ed almost feels like a protracted effort to put people off having sex rather than to talk about enjoyable consensual sex and explain what that means.

Of course, there are some too-rare schools that do provide brilliant, truly useful sex education. But whether your school sex education is cringe-worthy or not, you can pick up some good pointers on staying safe, not to mention free condoms. At the very least, you will find out where to go for more info. In the UK, sexual health services are free and confidential, and most local areas run special clinics where staff are trained to work effectively with young people.

People I interviewed also highlighted the fact that at school, we never talk about the emotional side of sex – it's all 'this goes here', but without a larger discussion, asking important questions like, 'what if you had sex with someone and they told everyone in school, how would you feel about that?' Aaargh, so much is simply jumped over because people are nervous about speaking about sex.

'Consequences' is one word that is inseparable from sex talk, and it's always underlined in school sex education. But just because it is a word you hear a lot, you shouldn't ignore it. Unfortunately the consequences from having unprotected sex can be really unpleasant. So no matter how much you think you know what you are doing, don't allow your precautions to get lax. Abbie, 23, told me that *'I've got a lot of friends who've got STIs from not using condoms, who now go "why did I do that? It was so stupid." At least they got tested.'* Talking more means we'd be able to think further about the effects of actions. And that could only be a good thing. I tend to think that the better informed we are, the better placed we are to think, plan and weigh up and to make active decisions about the things that most affect us.

ONLINE HELP

The internet is home to a bunch of ace websites full of fabulous information, guidance and genuinely enlightening facts about sex and relationships.

- **Scarleteen:** This American website covers everything from sexuality and STIs to the anatomy of pleasure.
- **Laci Green:** An unembarrassed, positive and informative YouTube channel – I learnt more from Green's 'sex+' videos than I ever did in school.
- **BishUK:** A British resource for anyone aged 14+ giving info on everything including how you actually can and can't get pregnant. It's run by Justin Hancock, the man with the world's best name for a sex educator.
- **Brook:** Brook is the UK's largest sexual health charity, and offers a range of great walk-in services, as well as online advice. They're also behind the Be Sex Positive campaign. They have been running for 50 years, so your parents will have heard of them, too.
- **Sexpression:UK:** A student-led network of projects based at different universities aimed at empowering young people to make informed choices about their sexual and reproductive health.

POPPING YOUR CHERRY, AND OTHER BIZARRE METAPHORS

I'm not a fan of the phrase 'losing your virginity'. It suggests one of two options – either something painful and tragic, or else very absent-minded. Virginity must be one of the only things people are pressured to lose (other than tacky Christmas jumpers, incriminating photos or unfashionable haircuts). Sex, when you're at the right age and in the right space, should be a gain, a positive new experience, a pleasure – not something cast off or mislaid somewhere.

Plus, we have some rather odd phrases for it: like 'popping your cherry'. What does it actually mean? We're talking genitals here, not balloons or bubbles. These phrases are perhaps a reflection of the fact that we are happier to rely on weird images over plain truth.

However 'virginity' is framed though, it remains a big topic. To get to a certain point without having 'done it' (never has the word 'it' had more stress placed upon it) is sometimes framed as shameful. Utterly ridiculously, it seems to suggest you're lacking a teen milestone until that darn cherry has been popped. 'Losing your virginity' also tends to only ever be framed in heterosexual terms, ignoring same-gender relationships, and suggesting some historical sexism left over from when female 'virginity' was a prized possession. Ooh, another tick on the 'woman-as-objects' bingo scorecard!

SEX: IT'S NOT JUST FOR HETEROS

It feels as though it ought to be unnecessary to even include this heading. Really, it is now a given that we happen to fancy different people, and wherever you sit on the vast sexuality spectrum, it's going to be fun. Whoever you choose to be with, it's likely to include lust, love, unrequited desire, heartbreak and dizzy stomach-flips. Sadly, though, there are still people getting het up about their fellow human beings' choices or sexual preferences. However, that shouldn't take away from the fact that your sexuality is a confusing, brilliant, complex, ENTIRELY personal thing. It is yours, and yours alone to own.

For me, finding out who I liked to date was a mix of new experiences, working out boundaries and re-negotiating who I was attracted to. It was about curiosity and nervousness, taking chances and missing opportunities, embracing spontaneity some days and making carefully measured choices on others. A whirl and a swirl throughout. Still is. I'm taking it one date at a time.

THE PANORAMIC PORN-O-RAMA

We live in a bizarre society. I mean, seriously bizarre. Sex is simultaneously everywhere, but still taboo in lots of ways. You can see all the tits you want, but honest talk remains as hard to find as a full-frontal view of a penis. What was once found on the odd videotape and in top-shelf magazines is now a mere click away. But we still don't seem to be able to talk about it.

On the other hand, there's a lot of chatter about the effects of porn. I still remember how disturbing I found it at school when the guys waved around porn clips on their phones, pushing them under our noses. It was either that, or groups of girls giggling over what they'd seen – trying to outdo each other in describing what they'd watched in lurid detail.

The words 'fiction' and 'fantasy' often come up when talking of porn. That it is *not* realistic is, hopefully, obvious. But maybe it's easier to recognise this when you're old enough to make the distinction between porn sex (filmed in a room full of people and cameras, with all sorts of expectations over how bodies and other stuff should look) and real sex (sometimes wonderful, sometimes awkward, and reliant – RIGHT? – on genuine communication).

Especially as a teen, when you're still figuring out your identity and sexuality, then some of those expectations that come with porn may have negative effects. I've already mentioned the assumptions I had about (lack of) body hair as a young teen … Pubic baldness aside, other friends of mine have talked about things they were asked to do that they weren't happy with – and one mentioned that her boyfriend didn't know whether female orgasms existed! I asked lots of people about how others view female sexuality as part of my research for this book. Beth, 17, said to me, *'People need to be told: number one) It's ok to want to have sex; number two)*

It's also normal to not want to do certain things because your one true love saw it "on this video once".'

The IPPR (Institute for Public Policy Research) did a survey of 500 18 year olds in 2014. One of the resulting statistics was this: 66 per cent of young women agreed, 'it would be easier growing up if pornography was less easy to access' – while only 20 per cent of young men thought so. This doesn't mean it's that way for everyone, but it does point towards some potentially difficult, damaging consequences. It is worth pointing out though that porn is often spoken about as if every single teenager is watching it, but there's still a sizeable number who have no interest in doing so.

So are the people who say porn is bad also implying that there is something wrong with sex? It's a confusing question, because some probably are saying that, but sex and porn are different things. Whatever your views on porn, they should not be confused with your views about sex. Amanda, now 20, said to me, *'The porn industry projects unrealistic expectations onto teens, and makes them think they have to act and behave certain ways. I spent so much time in my early sexual encounters worrying about how I should be acting, instead of enjoying myself.'*

For me, the key word here is 'acting'. Porn is a performance but in turn, it can suggest that sex is a performance, with 'wrong' and 'right' ways of doing things. That's a huge and horrible pressure to place on something that should be about shared experience and shared pleasure.

THOUGHTS ON SEXTING

The revolution in the quality and affordability of camera phones has led to some pretty interesting developments in the way people show their, err ... affection for each other.

A lot of the time when you hear talk about sexting, it's about when it's gone wrong – or, more specifically, when the shared content has reached a wider audience. As Philippa, 16, said to me, *'I know one boy was expelled and put on the sex offenders register for sharing a video of his girlfriend (who was quite a bit younger than him).'*

Sexting is technically illegal. When it comes to pictures of someone under 18 on a phone or computer, because the pictures/images are of a minor, they are classified as child pornography. The legal term is being 'in possession of an indecent image of a child'. If you share it, you're actually distributing what is considered to be child pornography.

However, given the potential seriousness of this content getting into a wide circulation, it is infuriating that the responsibility continues to be placed with the one pictured (usually female). Why on earth don't we place the blame firmly on the idiot who decided to make that snap public?

As unfair as it is that the responsibility is mistakenly placed on the shoulder of the victim, it's sensible not to send photos or videos. Just because you might be in a loving relationship and assume someone's trust, doesn't mean things won't change.

Throwaway actions can have long-term consequences. Whatever you send to one other person could potentially be seen by everyone at school, or further afield.

If the worst does happen, you are absolutely, totally, utterly NOT in the wrong. Please tell someone, and get help. *You* should not get into trouble, the shitbag who publicly shared your images should. Anyone who feels they deserve to see 'nudes' or are happy to show them to others is playing around with some very nasty power, and in need of condemnation.

SLAGS, SLUTS AND SLAPPERS: DOUBLE STANDARDS

The crudely drawn dick is an inevitable part of the secondary school experience, they're everywhere. But when was the last time someone sketched a vagina on a desk? More challenging artistically, you might argue, less easy to scribble in felt tip than a simple cock and balls.

As crude as it sounds, this seems to be an accurate symbol of a culture where male sexuality is more openly celebrated than female sexuality. The guy who sleeps around is congratulated. The girl who enjoys sex? Well, you choose the term. *Slut, slag, ho, bitch, slapper, whore.* I'm sure you can think of others: but none of them will be nice.

To look at it another way, there's an idiotic comparison that pops up now and again, which suggests 'a key that opens many locks is a master key, while a lock that opens to many keys is a bad lock'. But what the hell is that supposed to mean? For starters, the outcome can be easily changed by using other examples: A good pencil sharpener sharpens many pencils, but a crap pencil requires many sharpeners.

And why on earth are we judging something as 'good' based on what's being put in it or what it's being put into? That's like saying that a pencil that's never been used or sharpened is a rubbish pencil. It's not. It just hasn't been sharpened yet. It probably will be in the future when it has found the right sharpener. And enough about pencils already.

What such ridiculous metaphors demonstrate is that equating genitals with keys and locks or pencils and sharpeners ends absurdly. What the key metaphor really reveals is a culture of double standards: Guys get laid. Girls get judged. The fact that it takes two to tango doesn't seem to register. Obviously, this is a vast simplification, only taking account of boy/girl relationships, but it's worth picking up on.

On the other side of the coin, the word 'slut' has a cousin: 'frigid'. Opposite in meaning but similar in intent. Whether the insult is aimed at women sleeping with lots of people or a woman sleeping with none, there's a sense that these private choices are worthy of (negative) social comment. Girls are expected to be just the right balance of available and aloof. But whatever side of the line you fall over – too sexual, not sexual enough – both criticisms suggest that as young women, we're not quite attaining the level expected. And this level is never a tightrope that men have to walk.

Yas Necati:
The Campaigner

Yas is a student and feminist campaigner. Age 17, she fronted the demands to Michael Gove to update the sex education curriculum, supported by the *Telegraph* newspaper. Her petition gained more than 50,000 signatures.

Why did you start the Campaign for Consent?

I was talking to some friends – we'd just finished our GCSEs – and we realised how our sex and relationships education hadn't really prepared us, and decided to do something about it.

How did it get going?

We had loads of responses, particularly from teachers and teen girls. I think they felt the same way. We had one girl who made a video and went around interviewing lots of other people.

I know you also got involved with 'No More Page 3' campaign to get topless pictures out of *The Sun* newspaper. What did that involve?

I organised a protest outside *The Sun's* HQ. We made origami flowers and wrote messages on them about the campaign and tied them to trees around the building – then got chucked out by security. They just thought we were doing a workshop to begin with! I've also dressed up in costumes and joined flash-mobs.

What about the people who try and force your silence?

There's been a lot of trolling to campaigners I've been working with. I've had rape threats. I think it needs to be dealt with better - social media ignores a lot of what's going on, and it needs to be monitored so that if someone reports something, it's actually addressed. Trolls know that they can get away with it - they make an account, attack someone, and shut it down.

How did you challenge the status quo as a teen?

When I was much younger I'd wear boys' clothes and not care. Then I got to secondary school and went, 'I'm going to forget everything that's in my heart and do what others expect of me.' Then when I started identifying as a feminist I changed quite dramatically. In my school there was no one else interested.

Why do you think that was?

We still have sexist ideas of what masculinity and femininity should be. Most people don't like those ideas, but they go along with them because that's what society tells them they should be doing. If everyone disagreed with this and went this is nonsense - we'd be alright, yet we follow this system. As kids you question everything, and then you get to that age when you stop asking.

WHAT A LOAD OF ...

'Wank' was one of the most frequently heard words at my secondary school. Only among the boys, mind. They could boast and joke about it to their hearts' content. But girls masturbating? Those who did, and talked about it, were treated with a strange, unsettled kind of awe – other girls clamoured to ask them questions, then were often snide about them behind their backs.

Having an orgasm on your own didn't have the same status-reward as those who boasted about what they'd been doing with their boyfriends. Talking about bedroom antics that happened with someone else allowed those girls to assert their desirability. The same high-five wasn't given to a girl when it was just an individual and her own sexual pleasure.

In those first few years it seemed that many girls felt guilty or ashamed about their personal sexual experiences. There's very little out there to reassure the average 14 year old that what she's enjoying is very natural. Masturbating is a taboo that keeps most of us schtum.

Perhaps it is unsettling because it's an activity that has nothing to do with someone else's approval. It simply fulfils your own wishes/gratification/stress relief. There is still a weird stigma surrounding female pleasure, with or without someone else. Women's sexual gratification is much less visible in popular culture (unless presented from or for the male point of view: naked ladies being used to sell cars, for example, blurgh). In recent years there's been lots more open conversation, though, especially thanks to women like Caitlin Moran who talk frankly about female orgasms. Yes to this trend for frankness! Long may it continue.

WHY CAN'T WE JUST ENJOY IT?

One of the things I come back to again and again with relationships is just how much we view them in terms of our own inadequacies. Whether it's because you've never been in one, or you've been in more than you can count, there's always some cultural message suggesting that your experience is a bit wrong. It's the same with sex. Too much, not enough, not good enough, a bit 'weird' ... We're continually matching up our own experiences (or lack of them) with other people; all sorts of outside forces conspire to suggest that there's probably something lacking.

Which is silly because you're meant to enjoy both relationships and sex. We don't hear words like 'pleasure' or 'respect' or 'reciprocation' enough. When everything is good, exciting things should lie ahead. Getting wrapped up in flimsy expectations, the judgement of your peers, worries about performance and other etceteras means that it's easy to lose sight of that.

Whether they last forever or come and go, relationships are just another part of a big set of connections that multiply and change as you grow. Like any friendship, they should be an addition, another something lovely to add to your life.

8

WHEN I GROW UP ...

Age five I wanted to be a wedding dressmaker. I still have one or two drawings – thickly crayoned outlines of frills and voluminous skirts fit for a princess. As I grew up this morphed into wanting to be a fashion designer or maybe a fashion journalist – I kept notebooks stuffed full of sketches, fabric swatches and scrapbooked images torn from magazines. Then, when I was about 15, I flirted with the idea that acting might be the path for me. I set about reading lots of plays and collecting monologues that I'd like to perform.

But having surgery literally put me on my back. Slowly, slowly over the next few months after the operation shook up life for a little while – I switched directions again. Perhaps because I was out of action for a while, writing became my thing. It had always been in the background; my computer was full of half-started novel ideas and nearly finished short stories. Now it became a compulsive interest. I wrote pages and pages of notes, brainstorming blog articles, listing potential poems to work on, and sending the odd (mainly unsuccessful) pitch to newspapers and magazines.

When I decide I want to do something I pursue it intensely. So how do I stay motivated? What made me want to write and write and write when it still hurt my back to prop up my laptop on my knees? To me, staying motivated is about waking up in the morning and looking forward to what the day ahead holds. Now and then the odd day will be massively stressful or challenging, but I know it will be rewarding in the end.

So how do you hone that sense of excitement – of things to look forward to in between the humdrum of homework and other commitments? Well, perhaps it's worth asking yourself: what makes you tick?

I like the notion of ticking like a clock because it suggests motion and drive. Whatever gets you ticking is the stuff that keeps the minutes whirring and the hours rolling by at pace. These beats give you a sense of purpose, and maybe some structure too. They're what wind you up (in a good way!) and set you going.

It doesn't even have to be interests with concrete results or ambition attached to them. It's probably just what intrigues you most or gives you a lot of pleasure. In fact, plenty of the best experiences are those that don't have ACHIEVEMENT or THIS WILL GET APPROVAL stamped all over them. Finishing a really satisfying book and writing a mini review of it in your diary. A good day out and taking lots of artsy pictures. Giving your room a creative makeover (collages and pinboards galore). Anything that gives you a sense of 'hooray!' and leaves you satisfied when you go to bed. These are all awesome things to cultivate, and certainly do keep me ticking when other areas of life threaten to become overwhelming.

HOW TO SPIDER UP A PLAN 〰→

I'm a big fan of spider diagrams. I got through revision for most of my exams using them: quotes and facts and threads of thought neatly condensed into a series of interlocked arrows. List out all your talents and interests and see how they are connected, and brainstorm what you might do with them. Spider diagrams are great for finding out what makes you tick (or tock):

- Take a sheet of paper – the bigger the better.
- Put some words or a question in the middle: 'working out what on earth I'm doing', 'plans', 'sorting the chaos', 'getting my shit together', 'blueprint for world domination'. Whatever you need to plan.
- Branch out from the centre with whatever comes to mind: anything and everything that comes into your head when you ask yourself the question.
- Next, consider the spider legs in turn: what makes each point interesting or important to you? Give each little island offshoot ideas of its own.
- Divide, sub-divide, and sub-sub-divide until you are done. From your initial ideas you'll have trees and branches spidering all over the place.

The next day you can review your work and see what jumps out at you from the web of ideas: sometimes I'm surprised by how easily a spider diagram allows me to straighten out issues or spark new schemes. Allow yourself to just write and see what emerges.

DEVELOPING THE THINGS YOU LIKE DOING

One BIG advantage of being a teenager is having some space in which to experiment and play around with everything. We often think of 'play' as a word for kids, but I think we should all play more – mess around, make things up, be silly and spontaneous and less self-conscious. It really helps make decisions when you don't overthink them.

So set aside some time. Time to be stupid, time to be smart, time to daydream and time to go out and do stuff because you want to – and you can. You may discover along the way that there are a lot of things you hate, but that can be just as useful. It helps develop a sense of what you like and what you don't, what warms you up and what leaves you cold.

If you need help deciding what you like doing, don't forget all the obvious stuff about joining clubs or looking beyond school, bla bla bla. I could add in some further guff about 'being willing to take risks' or 'pushing yourself outside your comfort zone', but what does that actually mean, anyway? Where are the edges of that zone? Are you already standing in it? Is the discomfort zone a better place to be? Is it as well decorated as the comfort zone?

HAVE I FOUND MYSELF?

The phrase 'finding yourself' is a bit misleading. Is there a map, a set of clues, and a compass – needle pointing in towards the 'true you'? What happens when you do find yourself? Is it like one of the treasure hunt stories where, when the seeking part is over and the treasure has been located, everyone can pack up and go home?

Perhaps it's better to look at it this way: I don't think you 'find' yourself. I think you *form* yourself. This involves a similar set of experiences: discovery, exploration, adventure, journeying, dead ends and the occasional breakthrough. But why should there have to be a specific end point? The process of forming an identity is ongoing. It doesn't stop at a particular age, like you have a 'eureka! I finally know who I am!' moment. Instead it's a never-ending round of evaluating, treasure grabbing and re-assembling. Who knows what's ahead?

HOW TO START YOUR ENGINES

Is it all a bit much? A problem snarling up your aspirations? I'd be surprised if there wasn't, to be honest. Sometimes everyone needs a little booster.

Feeling shy?

Perhaps you know exactly what you're intrigued by, but hold yourself back. That's a hard one. Being anxious can really get in the way of doing what you love – and there's no quick-fix to banish the nervousness, other than acknowledging what scares you. So ask yourself: what's the worst that could happen? Don't scare yourself into submission, but work through in your head what you think is achievable. Don't beat yourself up if it still seems a bit out of reach. It can take a few years, and perhaps a change of age and scene, before you get there: but you *can* get there.

Lack of confidence in your own abilities?

Never let yourself believe that you are not good enough. I know that's quick and easy to say and hard to feel. But the beast that leans over your shoulder muttering things like 'look at what that person over there has achieved. You're nothing by comparison', has to be put down. You are enough. You are great. What's more, you have places to go. You deserve to do good things.

🌟 Worried about the future?

All too often the real world intrudes on all the things we'd like to achieve. Being pragmatic and thinking ahead is kind of helpful, but it doesn't stop you from pursuing lovely moments of wish-fulfilment in the meantime. Even it's just carving out half an hour in your day to do something you love.

🌟 Just finding it all a bit shit?

Life can be difficult. Anyone who doesn't acknowledge that is reshaping reality. Sometimes there might be things happening to you, or those you love, that make you feel out of control or a bit stuck. And that's fine. Being human involves experiencing those tangled, troubled times. But it also involves pushing for the things that matter and working out what keeps you going.

Juno Dawson: The Author

Juno's books include *Under My Skin*, *All of the Above*, *Mind Your Head*, and *This Book Is Gay*. They jump from dark fictional thrillers to non-fiction books that have resonated with countless teenagers. Juno is also Role Model for Stonewall, and (possibly one of the best titles ever) Queen of Teen 2014.

Your fiction books often have strong horror/thriller angles. Do you think there's something about these kinds of themes and stories that allows you to explore teenage experiences in a particularly intriguing way?

It's all metaphor. I mean, Joss Whedon made an art form (in *Buffy the Vampire Slayer*) of turning teen angst into 'monsters'. I only ever write books I'd have wanted to read as a teenager and, for me, that was horror and thriller titles.

You're (rightly!) very vocal on the fact that we need more diverse YA books – and, well, more diverse everything-in-general. Are we beginning to make moves in that direction? Or have we still got a long slog ahead?

There are so many diverse books now but they often struggle to reach the market. The issues seem to be industry-based ones.

I believe the publishing industry plays it safe – they gear up behind 'sure thing' titles and few others. I think they often sell lowest common denominator titles and authors in a bid to reach the largest possible audience which is depressing. That said, the publishing industry is FAR less guilty than film and TV.

You have a strong line in non-fiction books too – writing honestly about everything from sexuality to mental health. We need more of that. Is there anything you've found especially rewarding whilst working on them?

It's interesting because, for me, writing fiction is intrinsically rewarding because it's so creative and I get to spend time in made-up worlds. The rewards with non-fiction come later when you hear from readers. I get letters every day from young people about *This Book Is Gay*, far more than any of my other titles.

It was exciting to see all the support you received when you first talked publicly about being trans. You mentioned wondering what it would have been like if you'd been able to 'have your whole life in the right gender', rather than realising much later on. Do you ever ponder on what kind of experience you'd have if you were growing up as a teenager now?

It's all shoulda woulda coulda. Had I realised I was trans in the nineties, I'd have been forced to wait until I was 18 before they'd give me hormones anyway. Mainstream society so wasn't ready for trans people so it'd have been an uphill struggle. I'm so grateful to those pioneers who paved the way for now. If I was a teenager NOW I think I'd have had a better understanding of trans issues and absolutely gone straight past Gayville and on to Transtown. As it is, I had a wonderful time masquerading as a gay man so it's hard to regret too much. I've developed a deeper understanding of life and love that I certainly didn't have as a teenager, so I'm going into my transition certain of who I am.

I also really liked the way you talk about clothes – dressing up all the time as a child, wearing capes (I love a good cape!), watching your mum get ready to go out. I'm fascinated with the way that clothes change us, add confidence, allow us to play around with our image etc. Do you have any thoughts on that?

Gender is role-play for us all. The constraints of gender are felt by 100 per cent of the people on the planet and clothes are a part of that. Whatever culture you're in, however old you are, society tells you to do things based on something very arbitrary. The fun part is playing with the rules. The most fashion-forward individuals are those who challenge traditional concepts of what men and women should wear: look at David Bowie, Tilda Swinton, Grace Coddington, Kanye West, Jim Morrison, Chloe Sevigny, Bjork. No one ever got it right without also getting it wrong.

TAKE ADVANTAGE OF
YOUR TEEN YEARS

I'm automatically suspicious of anyone claiming that your teen years are the best of your life – what fatalism, suggesting there's some kind of ever-worsening spiral following adolescence. Surely it should be the other way round? Your teen years are the beginnings of things. So what's so great about being young? Well this stuff, for starters.

You can take risks
Ignore the 'general way things are done', and go ahead and do it anyway; whether that means dreaming big, or asking really-quite-cheeky favours from others. If things go wrong, you can smile sweetly and blame your abundant youth.

You've got hours to play with
Before the world of bills and rent rears its head, there's a golden window of time where you can look at what you like, and decide to work as hard as you like at it. You have time for trial periods to learn the ins and outs of whatever new skill you're focused on: treat any failures as a learning experience.

You can expand your circle of friends in all directions
When you are starting something new, it's good to find a mentor or two who can take you under their wing – people love to share their experiences with the next generation. These mentors will really help you believe in your abilities.

NETWORKING TIME

I love networking. On a basic level it's about knowing what you like, and talking about it with enthusiasm. To me it's about having an interest in other people's lives, rather than viewing people only in terms of what they can give you. If you're not great at talking about yourself, here are a few pointers:

- **Ask questions.** You never know who you're talking to, or what they've done. Being inquisitive will enrich your own knowledge and sense of the world, and may just lead to some interesting connections too.

- **Stay cool.** Mention your ideas to people in an airy kind of way – you never know what might come out of a passing chat.

- **Apply a filter to your contacts.** Seek out people with the same interests or who are already working in your chosen field and approach them for advice.

- **Show more things.** Always look to demonstrate your experience. Volunteer, become a hanger-on and create your own briefs and made-up projects so that you have something to show people and talk about.

- **Expand your zone.** Go to places where you can share your interests.

- **Keep some conversation-starters at hand.** An incredibly legit technique. I still do it now and then. Dream up some easy but breezy ways to begin conversations in advance, or turn up armed with questions that can keep a discussion going.

- **Find your heroes.** Go sleuthing online for people at the top of their field and see what they are doing and how they got there. Read their stories. Listen to interviews with them. Figure out what you love about their work. Gulp at the hours they put in, then rise to the challenge.

- **Enjoy.** Networking should be about the pleasure of bouncing ideas off other people, learning from those around you, and hopefully making good friends along the way too.

DO YOU WANT TO BE A WRITER?

Writing is a funny thing. Often I feel like I know nothing – at other times that I've got it reasonably sorted. I'm still negotiating this medium, but the more I feel it out, the more I love it, and the more I want to improve and refine it further.

Writing can also be hard. People tend to leave that out. It's amazing, oh yes, but tough too. Take this book for example. It started as a sprawling mess of ideas: a spider diagram or two, and a set of bullet points. Then sample chapters and detailed outlines started to flow. When it came to writing it, there were a few days of facing down a blank document – nerve-racking, knee-wobbling terror at the scale of work ahead.

I started with a loose first draft where I wrote and wrote with the adrenaline of a deadline pushing me on. Then paragraphs and chapters underwent major restructuring, whole new sections were added as it started to take shape. Further rewrites and discussions followed, and a round of tweaking as grammar was unravelled and thoughts condensed.

Those are the practicalities of structuring a big project, and you can apply them to most writing projects. There is a straightforward direction from plan to work – even if it doesn't always unfold in a straightforward way – that involves equal amounts craft and graft. Getting any piece of writing together is usually a mix of the amazing, frustrating, and time-consuming. But if you want to be a writer, you'll love it anyway (even when you hate it).

HOW DID THIS HAPPEN TO ME?

Before I started the book, I'd been blogging for about five years, and I'd had the odd writing commission too. One of the things that made it all seem much more possible was winning the *Vogue* Talent Contest, age 16. I'd been rewriting, editing and tweaking my entries so much that I only sent them off the day before the closing date. However, having entered before with no luck, I assumed nothing would come of it. I was shocked to find out that I'd been shortlisted, and when I picked up the 'congratulations' email on my phone I turned so white that my dad thought I'd received seriously bad news.

More than anything, what that win symbolised was a nod that I should continue with the writing. It was paying off. Being published in the magazine was a HUGE thrill too (seeing my words in print there is an experience I'll never forget), and I've written for *Vogue* several times since. I've also worked for lots of other places, and sent hundreds of unsuccessful pitches too. That's the reality of writing. An awful lot of it goes nowhere.

PRACTICAL MAGIC FOR WRITERS AND WORD WIZARDS ⁄⁄⁄⁄⁄⟶

In writing, there are five things you can do. Well, there are hundreds, and everyone will give you different advice. But you've got to start somewhere.

✻ **One** – Write. Write, write, and write some more. Be willing to show your work to other people. Revise and edit and return to work on it further. Then let it go. Allow it to have an audience, and a life beyond your laptop (or notepaper, if you're old school). Moving from 'not-so-good' to 'better' is going to require as much typing/scribbling/scrawling as you can fit in.

- **Two** – The flipside to 'write, write, and write some more' is 'read, read, and read some more'. Read anything and everything, and then question what you like and what you don't. Whose work do you admire most? Whose leaves you cold?
- **Three** – Be critical, and recognise when more work is needed. Read your work aloud, regularly. This will usually reveal a multitude of (small) sins like repeated words, overwritten images or long, baggy sentences. Also, never get complacent. Where do you want to go next?
- **Four** – Make your own chances. Pitch to publications (and expect some rejection). Begin a blog. Enter writing competitions. Network as much as you can, both online and in person. Take small chances in the hope that later they'll lead to bigger ones. Accept opportunities, even when they're scary. Build a name for yourself. Choose areas you're good at, and interested in. I write lots about sustainable style, among other things, and worked my way up from blogging for Oxfam to being featured in *The Observer* for my ethical outfit choices.
- **Five** – Be open and interested. Remain curious, get excited. What do you want to discuss, and in which medium? Features? Interviews? Articles? Poems? Plays? Short stories? Novels? Give it a go. It won't be perfect to begin with. But enjoy learning, and marking the difference in the quality of your creations over time.

Maybe there's actually a sixth point here – Every writer has their own way of doing things. It's easy to write about writing, packaging up personal experience as though it's the *only* way to go about it. But one person's perfect method is another's nightmare. Maybe some of what I've just said will be relevant, maybe none of it. You have to make your own rules.

OF GODS AND TEENS

In Roman mythology there's a god with two heads. Why? One head for looking forwards, one for looking backwards; both at the same time. Sneaky, huh? I like to think that's a good stance to take: looking back on what has been before, with plenty of looking forwards to what you would like to become.

Sometimes I get catapulted back to being a young teen. It can be a smell – a chalky foundation bringing back studios and cameras, or antiseptic hand gel transporting me to hospital post-surgery. Music also takes me back: listening to the albums I played on repeat on the school bus.

If I'm honest, I sometimes hated being a teenager. Be it getting stuck in the social games of school, or not being taken seriously, various things were ever so frustrating. But all of that is balanced by the chances I've taken, people I've met, opportunities I've sought, sketchbooks I've filled, hours spent tapping away on my laptop, and all those bedroom walls I've re-decorated time and time again …

These days I feel much more sure of myself, and what I'm doing. But two-headed god, am I glad I *used* my teens in the way I did. It wasn't always easy, and at times I felt stranded between several worlds, but it also gave me a head-start in a difficult industry, and so many wonderful memories. I'm not just glad to have got through it: I'm grateful for those years. I found a way of being teenage that worked for me – most of the time – and let me figure out what I cared about most.

Azfa Awad: ✳ ✳ The Poet

Born in Tanzania, Azfa is a performance poet and student. In 2013 she became the first black young woman from an inner city school to win the Christopher Tower Poetry Prize and subsequently worked as Oxford's Youth Ambassador for Poetry.

Do you recall the moment when you realised that you wanted to write?

I was in an English class, and we read Maya Angelou's poem, 'Still I Rise'. At that point I was still trying to fit a very Western perception. I'd wear what everyone else was wearing, do what everyone else was doing. With that poem I was like 'Wow – this black woman saying all this, I want to be just like her.' I began writing poetry. I showed it to a friend who loved it – she showed it to other people, my teachers …

What kind of advice would you give to young people who want to start writing poetry?

I think the first thing is just get some paper and start writing. Don't think about what it's going to be about. Otherwise you will get caught up in other people's perceptions of what a poem should be like. If you grab a pen and write, it will come from a pure place. And read others' poetry.

What do young people need to keep them writing?

Find someone to support and encourage you and give you feedback. I always had great teachers who were incredibly supportive, from when I first began writing for pleasure to when I wanted to learn new skills and editing techniques.

What do you find most satisfying about poetry?

Having an artistic mind means I am able to observe the world without taking part in it. Poetry allows me to capture it, which allows others to play a part in that observation. It's also freeing, even when I write about horrific subjects, as I am able to be vulnerable. Although it's an odd paradox, feeling comfortable while being vulnerable is liberating.

Do you draw from your own life experiences in what you write?

Writing for me is cathartic/therapeutic. It's a way of helping me make sense of the world and my surroundings. Writing about my experiences aids that understanding, as I'm able to not only express but reflect on those experiences; allowing me to learn and successfully move forward.

How does working with young people inspire and influence your poetry?

The power and passion that teenagers have inspires me to write about controversial topics; they teach me the importance of having a voice in society, and getting that voice heard; as well as speaking up for those who may not have one.

What kinds of things are you looking forward to developing in the future?

At the moment I'm working on a poetry collection, which I want to be published by Bloodaxe; so am looking forward to categorising my poems, editing and selecting. The rest of the poems will be going online as I'd like to introduce more people to my work – which is scary and exciting at the same time. So I'm looking forward to producing two poetry collections by the time I finish my degree, as well as a play and at least half a novel!

HOW TO FIND YOUR MOJO, MAYBE

You know that loaded question 'what do you want to do with your life?' There are plenty of people my own age who still cower on hearing it. Maybe you think you have no compelling interests and this causes panic. That's fine. Sometimes it takes a while to work it out. Here are a few possible avenues and routes.

Brainstorm what you're good at

This could be whatever makes you stand out, or what absorbs you to the point that you forget about the outside world. Could be academic, creative, skills-based, outdoors, sporting, scientific or something in front of a screen. (Am I sounding like one of those annoying tick-box careers tests yet?)

Take a mo to ponder

From social justice to languages to music to art to volunteering to knitting to farming to starting your own business. And that's just a random selection. Phew. There's so many incredible areas of knowledge and activity out there. Even just listing as many as possible off the top of your head could help.

Go back to your childhood

What got you going then? Did you have a burning desire to work on explosions, invent, or save the world? All of those can be translated into actual jobs or spare-time interests. Admittedly you may also have wanted to be a princess or a dinosaur, which are a bit less achievable as life goals …

✿ Think about what your family do

Is it office-based? Long hours? Flexible? Freelance? Alone? With other people? My parents are self-employed and often work from home, and I assumed that I would too. I've ended up following in their footsteps …

✿ Ask around too

From friends who have a few more years on you to aunts and uncles, people who are already working the nine to five (or emphatically NOT) can offer some fab insight. Choose the ones who'll be frank but fair. And perhaps don't ask them when they're grumpily stressed after a long day.

✿ Consider what you don't like

Sometimes this can be just as, if not more, helpful. Ring-fence off what you don't like, then let your mind run away to find the opposites.

✿ Give yourself a diversion

Sometimes you need to experience something brand new to get the inspiration moving. Pick a bunch of ideas and have a go. Trying something completely new can open up a whole new side of you.

✿ What about lifestyle?

Some people would have you believe that life is only worth living if you can earn £1,000 before breakfast ... but statistically that's going to be unlikely (and actually I don't think we'd all like that). Very few people actually make squidillions for little work. But, to ask a more practical question, does money motivate you, or do you just want to have enough to be content?

Question the status quo

Seems like the expected path now is GCSEs – A-Levels – University – Job. That may be exactly what you want to do. But if it's not, there are plenty of alternatives. Uni is not the be all and end all by any stretch.

Attempt small doses of bravery

If you already know what you want to do, figure out what might be holding you back, and come up with strategies for surmounting it.

Actually try it out

I get so frustrated with my sewing machine at times that I think I might burst. Tailoring clothes for a living was never going to be for me. But it took some experience to know that.

Know that decisions don't have to be permanent

We're living in a flexible world now where people move through all sorts of jobs over the course of their lifetime. Nothing has to be set in stone.

Expect the unexpected

You never know what lies ahead, or what opportunities may spring up.

✳ Katie Antoniou: ✷
The Entrepreneur

Katie founded a careers website for young women called Occupy Me. When she's not encouraging teens into interesting jobs, she can be found doing anything from journalism to styling singers to managing events to being a fab PR person.

What's the main focus of your website, Occupy Me?

The website is designed to inspire women to find or create the career of their dreams, whether they're teenagers looking at universities or career options, or at any point later in life where they've realised their job isn't making them happy.

How are you helping young women find the right job?

We focus on more unusual careers that you don't really hear mentioned – I currently know three professional hula-hoopers who have incredible jobs travelling all over the world performing and teaching. I think more people should be encouraged to turn what they love into a career.

Are there parts of the work force that are still men only?

There are jobs that are harder to get into if you're female – one of the women I'm featuring on the site is a pathologist, a career that for centuries was considered 'unsuitable' for women. There are so many incredible opportunities in science and technology, but women still aren't encouraged to work in these industries.

Do you think that there's a lack of clear information for young women trying to choose a career?

I do. I spoke to so many women who'd been encouraged to 'just go into retail because you're pretty' and similar horror stories. Or encouraged to go into the career that would earn them the most money, as if that's what's going to give you job satisfaction.

How can people find a job they really love?

One of the things I want to show is that if you haven't come across a career that you want to dedicate your life to, then work out what it is you're most passionate about, and create your own. There's never been a better time to be an entrepreneur.

Do you think there is just one perfect path out there for each person?

I think we need to move away from the idea that life is a straight path from A to B, where you need certain A-Levels to get to university, then you need a certain degree to get the job you want – and then you have to stay in that profession. It's all so restrictive. There are many careers out there that don't involve a set path.

SO WHAT IS IMPORTANT?

My favourite moments right now are where I'm looking forward, not back, where I feel the potential to come. It's a heady sensation when I'm aware of everything ahead: things to make, explore, do, achieve and, sometimes, fail at. That's the way it works: you win some, you lose some. Obviously I'm kind of terrified too. What if I don't make enough to live on? What if I can't translate what I love into a job?

But you know what? Right now, all of those questions are beyond my control. Some of them I can work towards, but plenty of them I'm just planning to dodge completely.

I'm excited for everyone in my generation: laughing at the silly stuff, campaigning for the big stuff, we are the most empowered generation – we own the internet, and social media has connected us like never before. The power and noise of young people is HUGE. Let's hear it even louder. We all have the capacity to go out there and do big things, stand up and be vocal, achieve, live fully. This is only the beginning. Plenty lies ahead – for all of us.

But in the here and now? Today. The future can be excellent or scary – it's unknown. Sometimes it's good to just enjoy exactly where we are. Perhaps that's not the most thrilling thing to hear. But I think it IS. It's about recognising that there's still a lot to come, whilst appreciating what's there already. About pushing ourselves, but knowing we're doing ok as we are. Life is about looking after ourselves here and now.

A MANIFESTO, OF SORTS 〰➤

In a book stuffed full of sentences, paragraphs, and chapters, I'd like to leave you with a round up of the things that matter to the fantastic teens and mentors who contributed to this book.

✸ Never Apologise for the Space You Stand In

You deserve to be exactly where you are, doing what you are. Your presence is important. It *never* requires an apology.

✸ Stick to Your Guns, and Be Polite About It

You have to fight for your deeply felt principles. You'll never be able to please everyone, and your worth is not measured in likeability. But fight your corner, and remember: good manners will get you places.

✸ Have the Right to Be Vocal

The flipside to that is recognising the validity of your anger at times. You have the right to be pissed off at injustice and stupidity and people who do awful things. Channel it. Fight back. Talk about it.

✸ Remain Curious

Read, think, do, experiment, and perhaps say 'yes' sometimes (and 'no' at others). Indulge in whatever you want to expand and explore further.

✸ Care About Other People

Actively support your friends and the wider community: part of standing up for yourself includes standing up for the rights of other people.

✸ Work Hard for What Matters to You

You'll get there. You'll get there. You'll get there. It may take time and setbacks and all sorts, but keep going. Have faith in your own abilities.

🌸 Don't You Pay Them No Mind

You don't need to prove anything to anyone. Anyone who intentionally or unthinkingly makes you feel bad is an idiot. They are not worth your time. Seek people who appreciate you for being 'you'.

🌸 Don't Overthink Every Little Thing

If you're like me, sometimes a worry will ricochet around your head endlessly. How long since that person texted? What about a particular comment someone made this morning? Why oh why did I make that decision rather than this one? Sometimes questioning is good. Sometimes it's an unhelpful use of brain-space.

🌸 Be Just as Fabulous as You Want

You can be as bright, bold and brave as possible – or as restrained and measured as feels comfortable. Whatever suits you. Own your style. Enjoy it.

🌸 Recognise that You Are Not the Sum of How Other People Perceive You

I stole this one from my friend Camilla because it was too perfect. It goes with ...

🌸 ... Know that Your Body is a Good Body

It is, it is, it is. Being comfortable and content in your own skin is a fantastic thing. Nurture it, if you can. And ignore the advertising bullshit.

🌸 Appreciate Your Achievements

You'll have your own to-do list, according to what's going on. Winning a prize? Overcoming an especially infuriating challenge? Just emerging

from bed and getting on with the day? It's all down to you. Mark each
step with pride. Mark it well.

✱ Allow Yourself Some Mistakes

We all screw things up from time to time. Give yourself room for being
stupid or mucking up. Don't punish yourself. You'll learn from it,
hopefully (and perhaps eventually turn it into a great anecdote).

✱ Enjoy Your Voice

It's there to be used. Speak up, speak out, speak back, chatter and talk
and bounce ideas and begin dialogues and generally make yourself
heard.

✱ And most importantly of all …

HAVE FUN. YOU DESERVE IT.

INDEX